HOW TO BLESS YOUR PASTOR

BOB BROADBOOKS

Stories of Uncommon Graces

HOW TO BLESS YOUR PASTOR

BOB BROADBOOKS

Stories of Uncommon Graces

BEACON HILL PRESS
OF KANSAS CITY

ISBN 978-0-8341-2551-3

Cover Design: Brandon Hill
Interior Design: Sharon Page

Library of Congress Cataloging-in-Publication Data

Broadbooks, Bob, 1951-
How to bless your pastor : stories of uncommon graces / Bob Broadbooks.
p. cm.
ISBN 978-0-8341-2551-3 (pbk.)
1. Christian life. 2. Christians—Biography. 3. Laity. I. Title.
BV4520.B66 2010
248—dc22

2010019780

This book is dedicated to the memory of Melvin and Margaret Broadbooks. They were the two finest laypersons I have known. I thank God for the privilege of having lived in their home for eighteen years.

CONTENTS

PREFACE

When the nurses finally allowed me to enter the recovery room to see Edith, I wasn't prepared for what I would hear. Edith was a wonderful elderly lady in our church. She had lost her beloved husband, Evans, a few years earlier, and now she had successfully survived a serious surgery. Through all of her struggles, Edith retained her feisty, tenacious spirit. You never knew exactly what she would say. She was refreshing.

Standing at the foot of her bed, I said, "Edith, it's me, Pastor Bob. They tell me you did real well."

Through squinty eyes, all she said was "Whoa! You've gained weight!"

I'm not sure if Edith was astute or anesthetized. I choose the latter.

A few days later, I entered her hospital room. She was sitting on the side of the bed. I heard her saying, "Lord, I'm tired. I sure miss Evans."

I said, "What did you say, Edith?"

Without a moment's hesitation Edith said, "I wasn't talking to *you!*"

Some laypeople keep the preacher humble. Actually, some laypeople keep the preacher laughing. One of the great joys of life is interaction with other Christians. These relationships are enhanced between the pastor and the laity.

Some laypeople keep the pastor blessed. I loved to visit Hank and Ruby. They were like grandparents to our children. Hank believed that every boy should have a fishing pole, so he gave one to my young son, Lincoln. The first time Linc went fishing was when Hank took him. I thought Linc was too young, but Hank didn't. "A man has got to learn to fish," he said. When you were at Hank's home, before you left he had to give you something—usually some meat from his freezer. To this day my children believe in the goodness and generosity of Christian laypeople.

Our daughter, Keely, remembers the artist, Clara, who gave her painting lessons. Lincoln remembers the golf pro, Nancy, who gave him golf lessons. Their mom and dad remember too.

I remember a gentle Christian woman who spoke loudly, even though I never heard her say a word. At four feet nine inches, Luella was short but fast. Her husband Alland was always saying, "Luella, if you'll wait up, I'll walk with you."

I guess if you had twelve children, you would walk fast too. Luella loved to feed people. Her favorite words were "Have you eaten?"

Periodically Alland and Luella would take a day off from their masonry business. They would go to the school and explain to the principal that the family was going to have an "educational outing" that day. The principal would therefore need to collect the twelve children.

They would go to the beach for a family outing. I said to Alland, "That must have been a great picnic."

He said, "Fourteen bottles of pop ain't no picnic."

Later in life Luella suffered a serious stroke that left her bedfast and speechless. She lived in that quiet world for four and a half years before her death. The family didn't want her to be stuck in a room by herself, so they put a hospital bed in the middle of their large living room. Luella continued to be in the middle of the family circle. She couldn't speak with her mouth, but her bright eyes spoke volumes. She had tenderly cared for her family; now they were doing the same. They were the ones saying, "Have you eaten?"

All twelve of Luella's children found Christ and have served Him faithfully. Evidently those children saw something genuine in their parents' lives. Some laypeople don't have to say much—their lives are all the commentary needed.

Albert Miller joined the church in Montrose, Colorado, in 1917. He was a rural mail carrier, and when noon came he stopped and ate his lunch under a tree. While he ate, he read his Bible. He found that by doing this he would read his Bible through every year. In Montrose Albert was known as a man of integrity. When the church was planning to construct a new church building, they went to the banker to see about a loan. The banker said, "Albert Miller is a member of your church, isn't he? If Albert signs the note, the money will be yours." Albert was not a wealthy man, but the banker knew that if he said something, it was true—he would follow through.

As their pastor, I had the privilege of witnessing a holy moment in the lives of Mr. and Mrs. Miller. Albert was gravely ill in the veterans' hospital, and I took Mrs. Miller to see him. After an extended visit, it was time for Mrs. Miller and me to return home. As we were getting ready to leave, I'm sure the two of them were wondering if Albert would die during the night. She bent down to kiss him. They hugged tenderly as they had done for sixty-five years. Albert said, "This might be the last time we say good-bye, Mama."

Through tears she replied, "Yes, Daddy, but we'll say hello in heaven."

I can't read the vignettes you've just read without tears. They're precious memories. So many great laypeople have affected my life positively that I wanted to write a book as a tribute to them. I wanted to write something that would be an encouragement and challenge to all the wonderful laypeople in the church world today who are trying to make a positive difference in their churches.

While in another book I wrote letters for pastors, this book is specifically for laypeople. In the following pages you'll discover qualities and practices that will help you be the best layperson you can be.

For more than thirty years I've lived in the parsonage. However, the first eighteen years of my life were spent in a layperson's home. Much of what I feel and think about ministry I learned by watching two tremendous laypeople, Melvin and Margaret Broadbooks. They were in my estimation consummate laypeople. They loved God with all their heart, mind, soul, and strength. They were concerned about their neighbors. They were faithful to every aspect of their church.

My mother served as the local missionary president until her eightieth year. For many years my father was the church treasurer. They served in every capacity at the church except pastor. They did their preaching at home, mostly through sacrificial giving and living. I've come to discover that in almost every church in North America there are faithful laypersons like Mom and Dad. Without them there would be no church today.

Pastors understand that their ministerial role is vital. They also know that the church can't function without an effective laity. Jesus knew this also. He poured His life into the twelve apostles. He knew that twelve men could do more than could one man doing the work of twelve men. If Jesus could have done the work by himself, He would not have bothered to gather disciples around Him.

The apostle Paul realized this truth also. In his letter to the church at Philippi, Paul speaks about the importance of preachers and laypeople working together. Philippians is often referred to as "the epistle of joy." But I believe that one of the sub-themes of the letter is clergy-laity partnerships. In Philippians 1:1 Paul writes "To all the saints in Christ Jesus at Philippi, together with the overseers and deacons." In this salutation he makes it clear that he's speaking not just to the clergy, the "overseers and deacons." He brings attention to the fact that he's speaking to "all the saints." He's speaking to the laypeople of the church. It seems to be an important clarification for Paul, because he took the time to make it clear.

In verses three and five of the first chapter of Philippians he writes, "I thank my God every time I remember you . . . because of your partnership in the gospel." Paul knew that the story couldn't be told, the needs couldn't be met, and the people wouldn't be reached unless the laity were mobilized in a dynamic partnership with the clergy. Throughout the Philippian letter he speaks to the laypeople of the church. Much of what Paul says is perfectly applicable to the laity. He talks about the practices, attitudes, and spirit of a layperson.

Overriding all of what he says is the idea that preachers and laypeople must work together. This becomes the basis for the chapters of the book you presently hold in your hands. Since Philippians is a letter for laypeople, the chapters of this book are letters for laypeople also.

We can do this together. We *must* do this together. Pastors and laypeople must work as a team. When we stop working together, animosities begin to develop, and the forward progress of the church is slowed. The pastor has personal responsibilities—he or she must preach the Word and administer the sacraments. He or she must also equip the saints and release them to participate in the exciting work of the ministry. As you read this book, I pray that you will be encouraged by the real-life examples of laypeople who are working for the Lord and enjoying the privilege.

One Sunday morning during the children's sermon, as all the children were coming down to the front of the sanctuary, I told them I was going to do an amazing thing: I was going to go all the way across the front of the sanctuary in just one step. I asked if any of them believed that I could travel that far by taking just one step. None of them believed that their pastor could do it.

Then I invited Rob Taylor to join me in the front of the sanctuary. Rob was a six-foot-six, three-hundred-pound offensive lineman for the Tampa Bay Buccaneers football team. With one step, I jumped into Rob's arms, and he proceeded to carry me across the front of the sanctuary. I watched the children's eyes as we traveled. They were amazed that anyone could carry their two-hundred-plenty-pound pastor that far. I noticed that by the time we got to the other side, Rob was panting pretty heavily. His thirteen-year professional football career ended soon after that. I've always wondered if I hastened his retirement.

Of course, the lesson to the children that morning was that we need the support of each other. We can travel farther in life if we have good relationships with our neighbors and with God. As I think about it today, I realize that this event was a parable about the Church. It was a layman carrying a pastor, and together they were traveling farther.

I have had the privilege of working with thousands of laypersons through the years, and my life has been enriched by them. Together we have made progress. I have felt their support and encouragement. Even though the burdens were heavy at times, they have continued to be faithful to the task.

In one of his letters William Jennings Bryan talked about "the man who was invincible in peace and invisible in war." Evidently the man was there in the good times but quickly filtered away when the going got tough. I'm thankful for a great host of laypeople around the world who are there in good times and bad. They remain supportive of their pastor and their church. You cannot pry them away from their responsibilities. You can count on them no matter what. This book is to pay tribute to them. I pray it will also bless them.

1. Gertrude's LIST

Yes, and I will continue to rejoice, for I know that through your prayers and the help given by the Spirit of Jesus Christ, what has happened to me will turn out for my deliverance.

—Philippians 1:18-19

Somehow I had made the list, and I didn't feel privileged. The phone rang at the parsonage that morning. "Hello. Is this Mr. Broadbooks?"

"Yes."

"Well, this is Mary Ann at the blood bank, and we need you."

"Me?"

"Yes, you, Mr. Broadbooks."

"Is there some kind of emergency?"

"Yes. There is a surgery, and we need your blood type. We've learned that you're AB positive. Only four percent of the population has your type, and we need you."

"Well, you see, I have this appointment at ten o'clock and then another one at twelve, and you probably wouldn't be able to work me in between those would you? . . . Oh, you would?"

I had never given blood before, and I'm not certain how they knew my blood type. But now I was on the list, and terror seized me. You see, I'm a chicken at heart. When I arrived at the blood bank, I was whisked into the drawing room. At least, that's what I would call it. They put me on a couch that looked like a dentist's chair, which didn't allay any of my nervousness.

I was trying to appear calm and in control, but on the inside my heart rate was up, my stomach was queasy, and I was screaming, "Let me out of here!" The nurse began to search for a vein. After several pokes that missed, she made a startling announcement: "You have skinny veins, Mr. Broadbooks." On any other day, that would have been cause for celebration. For, you see, "skinny" had never been associated with anything on my body before. But I was a little too panicky to rejoice just then.

Finally she turned my case over to a big fellow named Rodney. I guess he did the skinny veins. When he finally trapped one of those little guys, you would have thought he had just won a sweepstakes. I was not impressed. He said, "There. I got it! How are you doing, Mr. Broadbooks?"

Forcing myself to sound calm, I said, "Hey, there's nothing to this, Rodney. Doing just fine." I felt as if I would faint. I would still like to know how I made that list.

We spend our lives on lists. Some we like, and some we don't. We like Santa's list, the dean's list, and the A list. We work hard at staying off anyone's black list.

Let me tell you about my most important list. Actually, I have three. For many years, these have been vitally significant in my life. They are Gertrude's list, Margaret's list, and Carol's list. Each of these special ladies has included me on her list, and I will always be grateful. I speak of their prayer lists.

Gertrude was my college speech teacher. She was a praying woman. In fact, for three decades, if I had a serious prayer need, she would be the first person I called. I don't really know how I got on her list, but I know she regularly prayed for me. I remember one day when she told me that she had called out my name to God daily for twenty-five years. I was incredibly humbled by that. Just as Paul was thankful for the prayers of the Philippians and believed that they brought him deliverance, I, too, cherished Gertrude's prayers.

I have been on Margaret's list for more than fifty years. In fact, she prayed for me before I even got here. Mothers are like that. No matter what, through all the years, I've known she was praying. I'm fourth on her list, just after Melvin, her husband; Roy, her firstborn; and Anita, her second-born—then me. A mother's prayers are powerful.

When I married Carol more than thirty-five years ago, I finally got to the top of somebody's list. Carol's prayer list is actually a little book. It's very familiar to me, because it's always with her. It's part of her standard equipment—purse, makeup bag, book-bag, sweater, prayer list. Her prayer list is many pages long. Some of the items have been added and crossed out and added back again. She's quick to put you on the list if you ask her. I want you to know that I have seen the list, and my name appears first. That's a great source of comfort for me. I treasure her prayers. I believe, like Paul, that these prayers have brought much help and blessing to me.

As Paul wrote his letter of encouragement to the Philippi faithful, he mentions many admirable qualities found in their lives. One of the first he mentions is their prayer life. The prayers of these great laypersons had evidently made a difference in his life and the life of the Early Church.

Laypersons' prayers are no less important and effective today. You can pray for your pastor. He or she wants to be on your list. He or she needs to be on your list.

How often have you heard a sermon on prayer and you went home burdened? The pastor wanted to challenge you, but instead you were too discouraged even to try to be more effective in your prayer life. Well, just relax. This chapter on prayer will not do that to you. My prayer is that this chapter will be the most encouraging thing you have read on prayer and that it will liberate you.

You'll never think you pray enough—just relax.

I have had the privilege of pastoring many wonderful laypersons, but I can't recall any of them ever announcing that they had reached where they wanted to be in the area of prayer. I can't imagine any of the great saints of the ages saying, "I pray enough. In fact, I may have been praying too much lately." You'll never pray as much as you think you should. I give you permission to stop feeling guilty about your prayer life. Guilt is not a very good motivator anyway.

I'm not suggesting that you cease taking responsibility for your prayer life. Perhaps you heard of the Southerner who said, "I'm not fat—I've just been over-served." We must make an honest assessment of our prayer life and take responsibility for it. But your attitude about it is very important. I asked my elderly father how he managed to make it to ninety-seven years of age. His response was illustrative of a great attitude. He said, "It's not hard—you just shoot for 100."

What's your attitude about your prayer life? I know you don't think you pray enough, but don't let that debilitate your efforts. Shoot for more prayer in your life, but refuse to put yourself under bondage. You can relax about the amount you pray because—

You already pray more than you realize—just listen. I would like to suggest that you pray more than you think you do. So often we think that prayer is talking to God. It *is* that, of course. But it's so much more than that. Much of prayer is meditating on the Lord and spiritual concepts. Sometimes I'm moved in my spirit, and words pour from my mouth to God. But when I don't seem to have much to say, does that mean my prayer must cease? I hope not. Augustine said, "Prayer is not much speaking, but much listening."

Lloyd Ogilvie said that he once discovered he spent ninety-percent of his prayer time telling God what he needed and about ten percent of the time listening to God. His listening time usually followed his asking time. In an experiment, he started putting his listening time first and listened ninety percent of the time. Then he added about ten percent of his time in petition. He said he was amazed to discover that his prayers started to be answered more than ever. In 1 Kings 3:9 Solomon requests a listening heart. Why don't you join Solomon in that request?

Of course, there are many methods of praying that you can employ. Studdert Kennedy taught wordless prayer. With his imagination, he would place himself in a New Testament happening. For example, as he read the story of the blind beggar being healed, he would imagine himself as the beggar. He would see Jesus stopping to touch him. As he placed himself in that story, he wasn't saying anything, but he was praying. Thanksgiving and praise poured from his heart. Words were unnecessary.

Much of prayer is nonverbal. You don't have to speak to communicate. When I was a district superintendent for the Church of the Nazarene, it was required that Carol and I travel many miles. We soon discovered that we can ride mile after mile and not speak a word. That silence doesn't make us uncomfortable or nervous. The fact that we're not speaking doesn't mean that one of us is angry with the other. In fact, it means just the opposite. There's sweet communion in the quietness. Sometimes we reach for each other's hand. Sometimes I find myself looking at her out of the corner of my eye. Every once in a while when I look over at her, she's smiling at me. She may have been staring at me for a few miles and I wasn't aware. I can tell you this: we don't say much to each other when we're driving, but this is for sure—I would rather have her in the car with me than to go alone. We're communicating without words. And so it is with prayer.

My friend, you already pray more than you know. On your way to work when you were humming that chorus from the last service you were in? You were praying. When you thought about how good God has been to you? You were praying. When you were trying to decide how to handle that problem with your son? You were praying. When you were weeping with a broken heart the other night? You were not just weeping into the darkness—you were praying.

There was an old man who remained for hours at the altar of his church. He didn't move his lips, but it seemed that he was talking to God. The pastor's curiosity got so strong that he finally asked the old man, "And what are you saying to God?"

The old fellow said, "Oh, He just looks at me, and I look at Him." That, my friend, is prayer! I can think of no better definition for prayer than that: we just look at Him, and He looks at us.

It's true that you pray more than you think you do. But that doesn't mean you can't learn to pray more effectively. You can.

There is a simple little secret to prayer—just make a list. There are many mechanics of prayer we could scrutinize and put into practice. However, I believe the best thing you can do to enhance your prayer life is the simplest thing. Just make a list. There is something about writing down your prayer needs and keeping the list in a conspicuous place that helps you pray.

Have you ever noticed that there are some things you carry with you at all times during the day? As I write this, besides the clothes I'm wearing I have quite a collection of stuff on my person—a date book, a phone, a pen, a billfold, a handkerchief, a comb, fingernail clippers, a pen knife, a cloth to clean my eyeglasses, some mints, my keys, my watch, my glasses, and my wedding ring. I expect to use all of those things at least once today, and I want them close at hand. These are familiar items in my life, and if one is missing, I don't feel fully prepared.

You have a collection of stuff on you today also. Could I add one more thing to you? I would like you to add a prayer list. Put it in your date book, your purse, your pocket, or your billfold. Put it where you'll run into it every day. Make it part of your standard operating equipment. Two things will happen: (1) you'll become accustomed to keeping track of what God is doing in your life and the lives of your loved ones and friends; and (2) you'll be automatically reminded to pray. It's as simple as making a list.

Earlier I mentioned the three lists I was on. Let me update you. Gertrude's list is gone now. She passed away a few years ago. A great sadness came over me when I heard she had died. It was a selfish sadness. I knew she would not be calling my name to God as she had done so often. My life seems greatly lessened.

Margaret's list is gone now. She's almost ninety and suffers with Alzheimer's disease. She's no longer able to write, so a list is out of the question. But I still have Carol's list. I hope to stay at the top of her list for a long time yet, God willing. But as you can see, I need some new lists. Maybe I can get on my daughter's list. Maybe my son will start a list. I need to be on some lists. Maybe I could be on yours.

Pastors need you. They need to be on your list. If you could put them on your list, they would preach better, they would pray better, they would lead better, they would *be* better.

2. George's INTEGRITY

Whatever happens, conduct yourselves in a manner worthy of the gospel of Christ.

—Philippians 1:27

George Hamlin and his family were riding in their horse-drawn buggy one evening in 1913. They happened upon a large tent that had recently been erected on a vacant lot in Lincoln, Nebraska. There seemed to be a great deal of excitement, and their curiosity pulled them into the service. A preacher by the name of Minnie Ludwig was preaching, and George was captivated by her message. Although he did attend church, his faith was unfulfilling. When the invitation was extended, George left his seat and made his way to the altar. There he found Christ. He was changed from the inside out.

That night sealed my destiny also.

From that meeting, a church was organized in 1913. George and his family became an integral part of the church. Not long after that, they moved forty miles south to Beatrice, Nebraska, where George rented a farm. One of the first things he did was look for a church of the same denomination they enjoyed in Lincoln. There was none. He decided there should be one, so he began to pray. He also began to work. He did not realize that a layperson did not normally start a church. He was called by God to do this, so he forged ahead.

He located a storefront building in downtown Beatrice. He went to the bank to see about a loan. The banker asked what he had for collateral. Not being a wealthy man, George didn't have much to offer, but he believed there should be a church in Beatrice. The Lord had changed his heart, and he knew that God could do the same for many others in this town. The only thing George had of value was his herd of prizewinning Chester White hogs. The banker said that would be acceptable. George, a layman, a man of faith, a man of integrity, signed on the dotted line. He chanced losing everything he had in order to do what God wanted him to do.

George was a carpenter. He made the pews for the church. He remodeled the storefront into a lovely little chapel. There was no pianist available, so George played his violin to accompany the hymn-singing. The old saying was "Let George do it!" Since his name was George, he figured he was supposed to do it. He influenced many for Christ, including his own son, Howard, who became a missionary doctor to Africa. God used this wonderful man of integrity to begin a new church, and in 1916 the church was organized.

One year later, Albert, a widower, and his five children moved to Beatrice. Albert had lost his forty-year-old wife to cancer in Geary, Oklahoma, and they needed a fresh start. When they arrived, being Holiness people, they looked for a Holiness church. They discovered the church that George had started. So in 1917 the Broadbooks family joined the fellowship. My father, Melvin Broadbooks, was twelve years old at the time.

I've often thought about those events. How would my life be different if God had not impressed upon George the need for a church in Beatrice? What if George had not been willing to give himself and his possessions so unstintingly to see it happen? George was a layman. He was a man of integrity. He knew that his integrity was based on the integrity of God. He was willing to put his all on the line, because he knew that God would come through. God would take care of him and his family. George kept his word, because he knew God would do the same.

God continues to this day building His Church on laypersons like George. The apostle Paul was especially grateful for the laity in the Philippian church. He challenged them to be men and women of integrity when he wrote, "Whatever happens, conduct yourselves in a manner worthy of the gospel of Christ." Every pastor I know today is looking for people like this.

People of integrity do what is right. I read about two engineers who applied for the same job. They had similar qualifications, so the company gave the men a test to determine which one they should hire. Each man missed one question. The manager explained to the first applicant that they would be hiring the other man. He said, "Why? We both missed just one out of ten questions on the test!"

The manager said, "Our choice isn't based on the correct answers. It's based on the question you both missed."

The applicant said, "How would his incorrect answer be better than my incorrect answer?"

"Well," said the manager, "for question number five, the other guy put down 'I don't know,' and you wrote, 'Neither do I.'"

That is not integrity.

Paul says, "Whatever happens, conduct yourselves in a worthy manner." This brings honor to Christ and His Church. "Whatever happens" means just that. No matter what happens to you, make sure you do what's right.

When you have opportunity to give a bad report about someone in the church, don't. Do what's right. Keep your silence.

When illness or calamity comes into your life, don't curse God. Do what's right. Testify that you're going to continue trusting Him no matter what.

When a new Christian doesn't behave quite the way you think he or she should, don't accost the person. Do what's right—pray for him or her.

When Satan brings temptation into your life, don't succumb. Do what's right—flee from it.

In that church board meeting when you don't get your way, don't stomp out in anger. Do what's right—support the decision the majority makes.

If you don't think your new pastor is as capable as the previous one, don't quit the church. Do what's right—be supportive, and pray for a change in your own attitude.

When someone in the church says something about you that hurts, don't do the same. Do what's right—smile and keep going.

Many years ago a layman met with church leader Hardy Powers and went through a long list of problems he was facing at the church. Dr. Powers listened to his recital of woes patiently and attentively. When the man finally came to the end, he asked Dr. Powers what he should do. Dr. Powers just said, "Friend, do what's right." That's all he said. I imagine at first the man felt a little cheated. He probably thought, *Is that it? Is that all you have to say?* But for advice to be good, it doesn't have to be lengthy. Dr. Powers gave good, biblical instruction to the layman that day. Whatever happens, we must do what's right. People of integrity do what's right.

People of integrity are what they claim to be. D. L. Moody said, "Most people talk cream and live skim milk." Perhaps nothing injures the Church more than this. We claim to be Christian, but sometimes our lives don't measure up to the life Christ lived. We talk a good game, but the people who really know us know that we don't live that way.

I have a youth minister friend who told me something very interesting. One day he was talking to the youth group and asked them to write down on a piece of paper the hardest thing about being a Christian. He suspected they would say things like peer pressure at school or keeping away from drugs or sex or something like that. But there was an answer that repeatedly arose. What bothered them the most was that their parents did not live at home the way they lived at church. The teenagers saw a disconnect in the parents, and it troubled them. Mom and Dad claimed to live one way at church, but they were evidently living a secret life at home.

That same youth minister faced a difficult meeting one day. One of the boys in the youth group had gotten drunk, and his parents were very upset. The parents asked the youth minister to come to their family meeting so they could confront the young man. In the meeting, the father insisted that the boy tell where he got the liquor. The boy refused to say. The father insisted. The boy refused. Finally, the boy explained that he got the liquor right there in their house. It seems that the father had liquor in a locked closet and thought the boy didn't know about it. The boy knew where the key was, so he helped himself. As the boy explained this, the father turned crimson. My youth minister friend was asked to leave so they could resume the family meeting in private.

The story has a happy ending. The parents recognized that their hypocrisy was having an adverse effect on their children. Mom and Dad made their way to an altar of prayer soon after that difficult meeting. They asked God to forgive them and asked their kids to forgive them, and they poured out all their liquor. People of integrity are what they claim to be. They know that others are watching their lives, and they want desperately to "conduct themselves in a manner worthy of the gospel of Christ."

People of integrity do what's right. They're what they claim to be. In living like this, they bring honor to Christ. Someone has said, "Integrity is what we do, what we say, and what we say we do." Great laypersons have a walk and a talk that match.

The Rest of the Story

Twelve-year-old Melvin Broadbooks found Christ at the altar George built with his own hands. I'm sure George was smiling over his violin strings as he played "Just As I Am." Soon my father stood at the same altar and became an official member. Earlier there, he had committed his life to Christ and then committed his life and talents to the church.

When I came along thirty-four years later, I was privileged to enter a family that was still committed to that church and to Christ. Dad and Mom were laypersons of great integrity. They did what was right. At home they were what they claimed to be at church. They were involved in every aspect of the church. Dad sang in the choir when there was one, and Mom was always in the kitchen when there was a potluck meal. If someone needed to be picked up and brought to church, our car was available. If a Sunday School teacher was needed, Mom and Dad were glad to serve. They were the kind of laypersons every pastor depends on and thanks God for every day. Mom and Dad loved every pastor they had and tried to encourage each one in his or her ministry.

One early evening when I was ten years old, our doorbell rang. It was our pastor. Mom and Dad must have known the topic of the visit, so they told me to go outside and play. This was unusual, because I was always welcome to join in the conversation when the pastor came by. I think the pastor stayed about forty-five minutes. Eventually the front door opened and the pastor came out. He stomped down the front porch steps and stormed down the sidewalk to his car. He got in, slammed the door, and sped away. I thought, *That sure is strange. I wonder what that's about.*

Dad explained it to me sometime later. The pastor had gotten crosswise with some of the people in the church. He decided to leave the church and start his own independent church across town. He was going around to all the people in the church whom he liked and was asking them to go with him. When he visited our house, Dad told him that the Broadbooks family wouldn't be going with him. That's not what the pastor had expected to hear. He knew that Dad and Mom were some of his best supporters, and because of that, he thought we would surely go with him.

Dad taught me something through that experience. He said, "Bob, when I was a young teenager, I stood at the altar of our church and promised God that I would be faithful to Him and this church. If God told me to go with the pastor, I would. But God hasn't told me to do that."

Then Dad said, "Bob, preachers come and go. But the Lord is the same yesterday, today, and forever. We honor the pastor. We love the pastor and try to help the pastor. But we don't *serve* the pastor. We serve *the Lord.* We do what *He* tells us to do."

And for eighty-five years my Dad was a part of that church. He stayed faithful at the church where God had planted him. He didn't cease to be a member until God called him home and transferred his membership to the heavenly fellowship. For me and my siblings, this is a beautiful legacy. With integrity and persistency, my parents served the Lord in that little church.

Paul said, "Whatever happens, conduct yourselves in a manner worthy of the gospel of Christ." Friend, are you bringing honor to Christ with the way you live? Are you living in integrity? What the church desperately needs today are some more folks like George and Melvin. Would you be willing to take their places?

3. *Edith's* HUMBLE PIE

Do nothing out of selfish ambition or vain conceit, but in humility consider others better than yourselves. Each of you should look not only to your own interests, but also to the interests of others. Your attitude should be the same as that of Christ Jesus: Who . . . made himself nothing, taking the very nature of a servant.

—Philippians 2:3-7

It was an ugly car. It chugged up to the front door of the church in Montrose, Colorado, the Sunday we started pastoring there. It was a two-toned 1952 Plymouth. Actually, it had begun as a one-color car—green. Now it was a two-color car, green and rust. It junked up the décor. I thought, *I wish we could park that around back where not too many people would see it.* It didn't take me long however, to love that car—because of the beautiful woman who drove it.

Her name was Edith. She was a rather round and rotund elderly woman with salt-and-pepper hair. She had experienced a difficult life. Her husband had deserted her and the children many years before. Now, in her advanced years, she was still taking in ironing to support herself. I loved to go visit her. She lived in a tiny house and was always smiling and pleasant. Edith talked about how good God had been to her. Even with the pain of arthritis and many other physical problems, she was positive and encouraging. She had an upright piano in her living room that was painted sort of a speckled green. I guess she liked green. She would play, and we sang hymns together. We always got around to singing her favorite song—"My Wonderful Lord," by Haldor Lillenas.

Edith not only lived a humble life; she was a humble person. She, along with thousands of others, have followed in the footsteps of our humble Savior to embrace the church. In Philippians 2 Paul talks about the importance of humility in our lives. Every great layperson I've known and worked with had a humble quality about his or her life. Why is it so significant?

Humility decreases church conflicts. Paul says in Philippians 2:3, "Do nothing out of selfish ambition or vain conceit, but in humility consider others better than yourselves." It's not human nature to live like that. We're born wanting our own way. From our first days of consciousness, we think we're the center of the universe. We cry, and Mother leaps into action. As we grow older, that desire to be the star is still in us.

When you're handed a photograph of a group that you're in, what's the first thing you do? That's right—you search for yourself. It's human nature. But Jesus can change us. He can do a work of grace in our hearts so that we'll "consider others better than ourselves." It's possible for Jesus to do such a radical transformation in us that we will act and react not from human nature but from Christ's nature.

Can you imagine what your church would be like if everyone acted as Paul instructs? No one would have to have his or her own way but would seek Jesus' way. Everyone would be asking, "What would Jesus want us to do in this situation?" No one would seek to be the center of attention. People wouldn't get offended if they didn't get the solo. They would want the other fellow to have the lead part. They would live to "honor one another above [themselves]" (Romans 12:10). What a beautiful church that would be!

If you've ever been a part of a church conflict, think back about it. You can probably trace it back to someone who had to have his or her own way about something. Maybe it was the music, the pastor's preaching, the color of the carpet, the direction the church was going, or . . . The list could go on forever.

As I think about the church conflicts I've seen, generally people of humility are not involved. They just aren't interested in a big fight. They have more important things to do. I think of Rhea in Hutchinson, Kansas, and Marie in Tampa, Florida. They both worked in the church nursery, rocking babies for thirty years. These humble ladies really "rocked" the church. They wouldn't have been in the conflicts. It just wasn't their style. With Edith, they loved to sing:

I have found a deep peace that I never had known
And a joy this world could not afford
Since I yielded control of my body and soul
To my wonderful, wonderful Lord.

Humility increases personal happiness. Humble people are happy people. They've learned the joy of Paul's injunction in Philippians 2:4—"Look not only to your own interests, but also to the interests of others."

When I was a boy, the district superintendent in Nebraska was Whitcomb Harding. One day he gave some money to a man who needed help. The pastor with him said, "Whit, don't you know that guy will just take that money and buy something he shouldn't?"

Dr. Harding's response was beautiful: "Well, I'd rather be a sucker than a cynic."

I remember few people happier than Whit Harding. I think I know why. He was a humble man, and he looked out for others' interests. It's when we become isolated and insulated that we become miserable and morose.

Psychologists have been studying recently what makes people happy. They're saying what we Christians have always known but need to be reminded of periodically. University of Illinois psychologist Ed Diener said, "Materialism is toxic for happiness." Stuff won't make you happy. Being wealthy won't make you happy.

However, there are a few things that will.

Dr. Diener and others are now telling us that the happiest people are, first of all, not interested in keeping up with the Joneses. Happy people have discovered that life in a four-bedroom house is not happier than in a three-bedroom house. They know that if you were sad driving a Chevrolet, you'll be sad driving a Cadillac. A 1952 Plymouth works just fine. We know that those who seek to fill their spiritual needs will find joy. Those who try to fill their worldly desires will find only emptiness. Jesus taught us that when He said, "Blessed are the poor in spirit, for theirs is the kingdom of heaven" (Matthew 5:3).

Second, psychologists are saying that happy people surround themselves with family and friends. Sometimes people think that if they can just stay away from people, they won't get hurt and therefore will stay happy. The opposite is actually true. Happy people stay connected to others. It's the associations of life that lift the human spirit and invigorate our existence. Of course, there may be some hurts along the way, but Jesus said, "Blessed are those who mourn, for they will be comforted" (Matthew 5:4).

Next, doctors claim that happy people are busy people. They lose themselves in wholesome daily activities. The living of life in an active fashion will bring happiness. If you're busy, you don't have time to constantly check your happiness pulse. You're out among people, ministering and making your life count. You're bringing people together and bringing them to Jesus, where you work and where you go to church. Jesus said, "Blessed are the peacemakers, for they will be called sons of God" (Matthew 5:9).

Fourth and perhaps most importantly, happy people forgive easily. They don't harbor grudges and hurts. They're not interested in rehashing the past. With God's help they release quickly the injurious things people say and do to them. Her husband had abandoned her and the children, but Edith was way beyond that. She had long ago learned to give mercy and forgiveness. Jesus said, "Blessed are the merciful, for they will be shown mercy" (Matthew 5:7).

Jesus and Paul had happiness figured out a long time ago. Psychologists are just now catching on. Would you like to increase your happiness? Increase your humility. Let God order your life. Submit your interests to others' interests, and submit your interests to His will. Then y ou can sing with Edith:

I desire that my life shall be ordered by Thee,
That my will be in perfect accord
With Thine own sov'reign will, Thy desires to fulfill
My wonderful, wonderful Lord.

Humility stabilizes your reputation. Jesus was our great example of humility when He came to the earth. Paul says that Jesus "made himself nothing, taking on the very nature of a servant." The King James Version says, "He made himself of no reputation." Jesus wasn't concerned about His reputation. That wasn't His driving force. He wasn't concerned about what others thought of Him. He just wanted to do God's will. He laid down His own pride and in humility became a servant. Ironically, in so doing, Jesus stabilized His reputation. In His servanthood He became the greatest leader ever.

What the Church needs today is for laypersons to step on their pride and in humility pick up the towel of servanthood. Pride will destroy us. Isaiah 14 tells us that it was pride that caused Satan to be kicked out of heaven. Proverbs 6 lists seven things that God hates, and pride is the number-one thing mentioned. Pride short-circuits all that God wants so desperately to do in the Church and in our lives. James 4:6 says, "God opposes the proud but gives grace to the humble." I know you feel as I do. I need grace!

You could start a reformation in your church. You could renounce having to have your own way. You could announce that from now on you're no longer going to oppose the changes made at church that bother you. You could let it be known that you're going to support the pastor and the decisions of the church board even if it wouldn't be what you would choose. In short, you would "make yourself nothing." You know what would happen? You would stabilize your reputation. People's estimation of you would rise dramatically.

A single person can make a major difference in a church. One of the great stories of the Christian Church is the ancient story of Telemachus. He was a hermit who lived in the desert, but he felt that he should go to Rome. He found himself at the gladiator games in which men fought other men to the death. Eighty thousand spectators roared for blood. He was horrified by what he saw. He leaped from his seat right into the arena and stood between the gladiators. They tossed him aside. He came back. The crowd was angry for his interfering. They began to stone him, but still he stood between them.

Swords flashed in the sunlight, and soon Telemachus lay dead on the arena floor. Suddenly a hush settled over the crowd, for they realized that a holy man had been killed. Something happened that day in Rome, because there was never again a gladiator game. One man's death had cleansed an empire. This one man began a reformation, and his reputation lives today.

You may think of yourself as just one insignificant person in the church who would be unable to change things. But lying within you is the seed of great potential. You can bring about a reformation in your church if you'll live in humility. Humility is winsome. It's attractive. It's irresistible. There are hundreds of thousands of laypersons around the world who live like this. They're not famous. But they are faithful. Are you in that number?

All the talents I have I have laid at Thy feet;
Thy approval shall be my reward.
Be my store great or small, I surrender it all
To my wonderful, wonderful Lord.

It was my responsibility to officiate at Edith's funeral. It was a celebration. A dear saint had made her way home. We sang "My Wonderful Lord" at the service, and we all cried as we did.

The next Sunday I found myself missing an old, rusted 1952 Plymouth. As mentioned earlier, the first Sunday I was there I was embarrassed to find it parked right in front of the church. The first Sunday after Edith's funeral, I would have been happy to see it there, because that old car represented the life of a beautiful, humble layperson.

Isn't it interesting? The people who think they're the least among us often leave the biggest holes when they're gone. Humble folks are like that. They always point our attention away from themselves and onto a great Savior.

Thou art fairer to me than the fairest of earth,
Thou omnipotent, life giving Word.
O Thou Ancient of Days, Thou are worthy all praise,
My wonderful, wonderful Lord.

My wonderful Lord, my wonderful Lord,
By angels and seraphs in heaven adored!
I bow at thy shrine, my Savior divine,
My wonderful, wonderful Lord.

4. Ken AND Jean's ATTITUDE

Your attitude should be the same as that of Christ Jesus. . . . Do everything without complaining or arguing.

—Philippians 2:5, 14

Have you ever noticed that some laypeople seem to have a great attitude in every situation? No matter how difficult it may be, they seem to have the right outlook. My father was only two weeks shy of his ninety-eighth birthday when he died. He spent his last few months in a nursing home. He had just a few wisps of white hair around the edges of his bald head. He had only three teeth left and was not at all interested in securing any false teeth. He was unable to walk. He had to be helped into bed and out of bed. A few weeks before he passed away, I asked him how he was doing. His response was immediate. He said, "Everything's coming my way."

I'm not sure I could be that positive in a similar situation. But my Dad didn't think about complaining. It was not a normal part of his life. He was not overly delighted with his surroundings, but he would not tell you so. He really believed that everything of true value was coming his way. His stay in the nursing home *was* just a temporary stop on the way to his final destination.

Is that the way you are? Or are you more like the lady I read about? Years ago, Paul C. Smith was heading up *Collier's* magazine. In the days just before it folded, he called a full staff meeting to explain why the ship was sinking. Everyone came, including the stenographers and mailroom people.

In the meeting Smith held nothing back. He told of *Collier's* six-million-dollar debt and falling sales. He talked about the fact that they needed to somehow raise two million dollars. He talked for three hours. At the end he said, "And that's the fix we're in. Now are there any questions?"

A secretary from the back of the room said, "Yes—why can't the Schrafft's coffee wagon come up to the thirteenth floor?"

Some people are like that. They're oblivious to the big picture. They see life only as it affects them. Their immediate, natural reaction is to complain and find fault.

Your pastor knows this all too well. When the phone rings and he or she hears who's on the other end of the line, your pastor generally knows immediately how the conversation will go. The pastor knows if the person is going to complain or bless. Some people raise the pastor's blood pressure, and some lower it. Which kind of layperson are you? When the pastor knows that you're calling, will he or she relax or tense up? Every layperson has an attitude, and I pray that yours is the attitude of Christ.

It's been my happy privilege to pastor hundreds of laypeople, and most of them had great attitudes. I think of a smiling Sunday School teacher in Montrose, Colorado, named Charlene who had as her mission in life to build a dynamic young adult class. And she did it, because she had a you-can't-stop-me-and-God kind of attitude. I think of a gentle physician in Tampa named Joel who was willing to make house calls at three in the morning if needed. There were no complaints from him, just happiness about being able to serve. I think about a good man in Hutchinson, Kansas, named Phil who, though a successful businessman, had no greater joy and excitement than to see his church move forward. Laypersons like these are a great blessing to the pastor.

Henry Ward Beecher said, "There are persons so radiant, so genial, so kind, and so pleasure-bearing that you instinctively feel in their presence that they do you good, whose coming into a room is like the bringing of a lamp there." I want to be a person like that. I want you to be like that. Your pastor will be so blessed if you are. When your pastor is with you, I pray that he or she will feel that you're "doing him [her] good."

The apostle Paul knew about this. There were some who were a blessing to him and some who were a bane. As you read his letters, it's obvious. Some folks discouraged him. Demas and Crescens deserted him (2 Timothy 4:10). Alexander the metalworker did him harm, and Paul told Timothy to avoid him (2 Timothy 4:14-15). There were others who blessed him, like Timothy and Epaphroditus (Philippians 2:19-30). These were such a blessing to him that he wanted to send them to the Philippi Christians to lift them. They would be like "bringing a lamp" into their lives.

Paul says that we should adopt the same attitude of Christ and at the same time avoid attitudes that are an antithesis of Him. This is good advice for laypersons. We consider the negative first.

Avoid the sour attitude. "Do everything without complaining or arguing" (Philippians 2:14). Everything? Paul must be kidding. There are a few things we like to complain about. After four straight days of rain, we find it easy to wish for some sun. Don't you want to complain just a little when you see how much money the Internal Revenue Service is taking out of every check? Then there's the pastor's sermon. They seem to be getting longer. And that dear lady who sings at church—she always picks a song that's higher than she can sing, and the last note is flat every time. By the way, do we *have* to stand up while we sing all those choruses?

Evidently they had complainers and arguers even in the Early Church. It's been going on for centuries. It's human nature to want your own way. It's natural to be critical and faultfinding. That's why we so desperately need the mind and attitude of Christ. Without Him we become painful people.

Dryden said, "Everyone is eagle-eyed to see another's faults and deformity." If we could just rise above a spirit of criticism, we would take a giant step toward God. When a Christian senses that there's a distance between himself or herself and the Lord, it's often because the person has allowed himself or herself to become negative and critical. This just isn't Jesus' style. He's not critical—He's compassionate.

Jesus talks to us about being critical in Matthew 7:1-5—

> Do not judge, or you too will be judged. For in the same way you judge others, you will be judged, and with the measure you use, it will be measured to you. Why do you look at the speck of sawdust in your brother's eye and pay no attention to the plank in your own eye? How can you say to your brother, "Let me take the speck out of your eye," when all the time there is a plank in your own eye? You hypocrite, first take the plank out of your own eye, and then you will see clearly to remove the speck from your brother's eye.

Jesus gives us two reasons we should avoid being critical. First, it's dangerous and leads to your own judgment. The Phillips translation of verse two is sobering: "You will be judged by the way you criticize others." Jesus was gentle with the weak. He was strict with those who were guilty of having a critical spirit. The second reason Jesus gives for not being critical is that it is inconsistent and hypocritical. The chances are good that we are as flawed as what and whom we are criticizing.

"Criticism comes easier than craftsmanship". So said Zeuxis around 400 B.C. Michelangelo was once asked to judge another person's painting. The artist he was judging was far inferior to Michelangelo. But he just pointed out some of the good features of the man's work. Another painter who witnessed this accused Michelangelo of not being honest in his criticism—to which the great artist replied, "I criticize by creating." In other words, he didn't have to be critical. He would let his life and work speak.

Your pastor probably receives plenty of criticism. You would be such a blessing to him or her if you would refrain from it. Rabbi and comic Robert Alper told about a synagogue that used voicemail. He phoned and heard this message: "Welcome to Temple Beth Shalom. If you are calling from a touch-tone phone and would like membership information, press one. For our service schedule, press two. To complain to the rabbi, press three. To complain *about* the rabbi, press four, five, or six."

That's the way your pastor feels some days. It seems that he or she cannot please anyone. Our churches need more laypeople who refuse to complain and criticize and argue. We could accomplish so much more if we could just focus on our task of reaching lost people.

I'm not sure who said it first, but it certainly is true: "Some laypeople make pastors happy wherever they go, and some laypeople make pastors happy *whenever* they go." I challenge you to be one of the former and not the latter. Paul says there's a sour attitude to avoid, and there's also a better attitude to adopt.

Adopt the supreme attitude. In Philippians 2:5 Paul says, "Your attitude should be the same as that of Christ Jesus." We must adopt the mind or attitude of Christ. Great laypeople think like Jesus thinks. They don't have time or energy to get caught up in church arguments. They're too big to develop a spirit of criticism. They want to live like Jesus.

Paul tells us what the attitude of Christ is. It is found in Philippians 2:7-8: "[He] made himself nothing, taking the very nature of a servant, being made in human likeness. And being found in appearance as a man, he humbled himself and became obedient to death—even death on a cross!" Three key words here describe the attitude of Christ—"servant," "humble," and "obedient." He was a servant. He didn't come to be served; He came to serve. He was humble. He wasn't concerned about His reputation. He was committed to being obedient to whatever God asked of Him, even if it meant dying on a cross.

If you're serious about having the attitude of Christ, this is how you'll think. This is what you'll do. Complaining and criticism will be beneath you. You'll have more lofty atmospheres in which to operate. Your joy will not come from tearing someone down. Building someone up will energize you. You won't be scheming to get a different pastor who will serve you better. You'll be looking for ways to become a better servant to your pastor and anyone else you can help.

The only complaint heard coming from your mouth will be *O Lord, I'm not worthy of the privilege to represent you in this world.* Your satisfaction will be to do the will of God, no matter the cost. Your prayer will be *Dear Lord, make me obedient without reservation to your will.* Then you'll have the attitude of Christ.

This kind of attitude is not natural. The only possibility for you to have this attitude is for a supernatural work to be done in your mind. In Romans 12:2 Paul writes, "Be transformed by the renewing of your mind." Your life is changed from the inside out. You need God to help you change. You can't decide, *Well, I'm going to think happy thoughts for six months, and then I'll be changed.*

No, you need God to transform you on the inside. If you sense a spirit of criticism has invaded your life, run to Christ. Confess your waywardness, and beg His forgiveness. You don't have to live in spiritual limbo anymore. He wants to renew your attitude. Let Him.

Then you'll have to add your own discipline to the process. You may have to change some of your associations. You may not be able to remain a part of that little clique at church that tends to be critical and faultfinding. That just won't fit you anymore. You have the mind of Christ.

I read about a man who had the attitude of Christ. People said that when they were with him they somehow forgot about him and thought about Christ. I wish people said that about you and me. This man had a secret, one that all of us could use. Through the years he had read regularly some portion of Matthew, Mark, Luke, or John. Those, of course, are the books that tell about the experiences of Christ. As he read these stories about Christ, he pictured himself as being present when they happened. He thought of himself as a personal friend of Jesus, actually walking with him on those dusty streets. He imagined the dust swirling around his sandaled toes.

As he read those books over and over, he became familiar with every detail of Christ's life. He came to know Christ better than he knew any other man. He thought of Christ as being with him at all times. Whenever he had a decision to make, he would whisper, "Jesus, what shall we do here?" And he would know what to do. Little by little, the mind of Christ took possession of his mind, and he developed the attitude of Christ. And people said that when they were with him, they forgot about him and thought about Christ. *O Lord, help us be like that.*

This is the supreme attitude to adopt. If we can just let the attitude of Christ captivate our minds, our living and our dying will speak eloquently of the power of God.

This was true for Ken and Jean Chaney. Ken was 75, and Jean was 68. They lived in California. One day they got lost in a snowstorm in the Sierra National Forest. Ken Gross told their captivating story in *People* magazine. They were trapped in their car for eighteen days, and on envelopes and scraps of paper Jean wrote a diary to her children and grandchildren. She wanted to remain brave and positive. That diary is a treasured gift to the family.

> *Friday, March 1, 1991, 6:30* A.M. *Well, here we are in a winter wonderland! We have been here since about 6 or 6:30 last night. We skidded into a snowdrift on the wrong side of the road and couldn't get out. And then it snowed about another foot during the night. I can't even get my door open. (Don't mind the writing—I have to write on my hand and lap.) So many things I want to say. I want you all to enjoy your life and remember what is so dreadful today will be forgotten next year. Please be a family! And let my grandchildren know that I love them. . . .*
>
> *We began to realize that we were on a road that isn't maintained during the winter. Truly a miracle if anyone comes by. We spent the night singing hymns . . . and quoting Bible verses and catnapping. We would run the heater*

for about five minutes every couple of hours. We have no idea what lies ahead . . . so here we are, completely and utterly in God's hand! What better place to be!

They didn't find Ken and Jean for eight weeks. They surmise that Ken wouldn't have gone for help because he wouldn't leave Jean there alone. The diary continues:

The third day, and so far we aren't hungry. Found two little packages of jelly and a stick of gum in the glove compartment. Saving them. We reach out the window and eat snow. Daddy is feeling bad about not showing up at work this morning.

Monday, March 4. It is pouring rain. We're wondering if anybody has missed us yet. We thought maybe there would be helicopters or snowmobiles looking. . . . I wish I had more paper. I would like to write to each of you individually.

March 6, Wednesday. This will be our seventh night here. The gas is all gone, so no more heat. We have eaten one little packet of jelly between us. Rolaids and Tic-Tacs. Quite a feast!

The cold had frozen the windows shut, and for water they scraped the frost off the glass.

March 12. A drink of water for me will never go unappreciated again. And a bite of food—any kind. Today is the first day that I have noticed any weakness. I love you all. . . .

Kids: I can't find the dome light—writing by glove compartment light. Dad went to the Lord at 7:30 this evening, March 18. It was so peaceful, I didn't even know he left. The last thing I heard him say was "Thank the Lord." I think I'll be with him soon. . . . So much to say and so little time. I can't see. Bye. I love you.

She said, "We are . . . in God's hand. What better place to be!" Ken and Jean Chaney knew that the worst thing in life wasn't dying with Jesus. It was living without Him. They lived with the attitude of Christ. They lived as humble servants, obedient even unto death. And Jesus gently took them home.

I ask the same question with which I began: Have you ever noticed that some laypeople seem to have a great attitude in every situation?

5. *Roy's* HEALTHY LIFESTYLE

So that you may become blameless and pure, children of God without fault in a crooked and depraved generation.

—Philippians 2:15

Hopelessly addicted to heroin for fifteen years, Kurt Cobain sat writing a long letter to his wife and one-year-old daughter. He had led the alternative rock group Nirvana. The group had received many accolades for its music, traveled all over the world, and become a household name among rock music lovers. On April 5, 1994, he found himself in his Seattle home, emaciated in body and exhausted in spirit. He had been in and out of treatment centers and was now tired of fighting the drugs. He wrote, "I don't know where I'm going. I just can't be here anymore."

Tragically, Kurt Cobain represents people trapped in this "crooked and depraved generation." They don't know where they're going, but they can't stand to stay here anymore. Life seems horribly meaningless.

A number of years ago, *Life* magazine devoted an issue to answering the question "What is the meaning of life?" They interviewed hundreds of famous and not-so-famous people. They heard some interesting and unusual answers. Author Tom Robbins answered the question this way: "Our mission is to jettison those pointless preoccupations and take on again the primordial cargo of inexhaustible ecstasy." I have no idea what that means. Another author said, "Since age two, I've been waltzing up and down with the question of life's meaning, and I'm obligated to tell you that the answer changes from week to week." That answer is off course.

José Martínez, a cab driver, said this: "We're here to die. Just live and die. The only cure for the world's illness is nuclear war. Wipe out everything and start over." I don't think I would want to ride in his cab—he sounds dangerous.

Willie Nelson, singer and song writer, said, "Matthew 5:48 says, 'Be ye perfect therefore, as your father which is in heaven is perfect.' The purpose of life is to reach perfection. To achieve perfection, man must return again and again through many incarnations to conquer greed, jealousy, disease, anger, hatred, and guilt."

I think Willie's headband and ponytail are too tight.

Leonard Nimoy, Mr. Spock from *Star Trek,* said, "I find the question 'Why are we here?' typically human. I'd suggest, '*Are* we here?' is a more logical question."

I think Leonard wore those pointy ears too long!

Today effective laypersons have been able to sort through this "crooked and depraved generation" and discover what the true meaning of life is. They've believed that God has something to say about this in His Word. They've listened, experienced transformation, and have discovered the ultimate healthy lifestyle of entire sanctification.

Years ago while speaking at the centennial anniversary of Wheaton College, Billy Graham declared that among professed Christians, "sanctification is one of the most neglected truths in the entire Scriptures."

Preachers spend much time talking about the importance of being born again, and rightly so. But they must not refrain from talking about the fact that there is a second work of grace that can establish the Christian. The words *pardon, justify,* and *forgive* occur 194 times in the Bible. But the words *perfect, upright,* or *sanctify* occur 990 times, and around 500 times those words are applied to an experience we can enjoy in this life.

If the Bible places this much emphasis on a concept, it must be important.

The apostle Paul often uses the words *pure* and *blameless* to describe the life of entire sanctification. In Philippians 2:15 he says, "So that you may be blameless and pure, children of God without fault in a crooked and depraved generation." He used it earlier in Philippians 1:9-11—"And this is my prayer: that your love may abound more and more in knowledge and depth of insight, so that you may be able to discern what is best and may be pure and blameless until the day of Christ, filled with the fruit of righteousness that comes through Jesus Christ—to the glory and praise of God." There must be something important about those two words *pure* and *blameless.* He says it again in 1 Thessalonians 3:13—"May He strengthen your hearts so that you will be blameless and holy in the presence of our God and Father when our Lord Jesus comes with all His holy ones." Again in 1 Thessalonians 5:23, he uses the concepts together when he says, "May God himself, the God of peace, sanctify you through and through. May your whole spirit, soul and body be kept blameless at the coming of our Lord Jesus Christ."

The great laypersons with whom I have had the privilege of working have discovered the liberating and empowering truth of being pure and blameless. They have discovered that to live this ultimate healthy lifestyle they didn't have to become monks, live in caves, shun society, shave their heads, and cut themselves. All they had to do was surrender their lives, unreservedly, to a loving Heavenly Father who desperately wants to do this holy work in their hearts. They finally realized that they were powerless to make themselves pure and blameless. The heavenly physician would have to bring the healing.

These great laypersons tired of living the Christian life in their own strength. They grew weary of inner struggles and battles. In desperation they fell at Jesus' feet and cried out, *O Lord, make me pure and blameless. You do this desired work in me. I can go no farther without the fullness of this blessing!* Laypersons all over this world have discovered these two important truths: God can make you pure, and God can keep you blameless.

God can make you pure. Most born-again Christians tire of trying to live the Christian life. The ideal presented by pastors is exhausting to try to execute. They would like to "love everybody," but there's that one guy at church who really gets on their nerves. They would like for Bible reading and prayer time to be a delight, but mostly it's a guilt-filled requirement. They really would like to "love God with all their hearts and souls and minds," but there's a part of them that's still enamored with having their own way. The beautiful ministry of Christ to feed the hungry, heal the sick, and visit the imprisoned seems to be an ideal that they never quite reach.

But Christians don't have to struggle like this. You don't have to be frustrated in your walk with the Lord. God has the answer. He wants to transform you; He wants to change your essence so that you can live out the principles of Christ. He can make you pure.

The Greek word for *pure* is *katharos,* which is where we get our word *catharsis* or *cleansing.* God can cleanse you deep within. Samuel Logan Brengle was holding a Holiness meeting in which he talked about the cleansing power of God. Following the message, an earnest Christian lady came to him and said, "Mr. Brengle, if you had called what you were preaching about this afternoon 'consecration,' we could all have agreed with you."

Kindly but firmly he replied, "Ma'am, I was not preaching about consecration this afternoon. I was preaching about sanctification. There is as much difference between these two as there is between heaven and earth, as there is between a divine and human work."

Consecration is what *we* do. Entire sanctification is what *God* does in response to our sacrifice. He purifies and cleanses our hearts by faith (Acts 15:8-9). You can't purify your own heart. You can't do enough good works. No amount of volunteer service or giving will cleanse your heart. Only God can make you pure.

We were meant to live like this. We were originally created this way before the fall of Adam and Eve in the Garden of Eden. We were designed for this purity. After the fall, humanity was bent and twisted by sin. Since the fall, you and I have lived with a debilitating infection. We have a low-grade fever, a weakness, a loss of energy and strength. We function at a reduced capacity and efficiency. But God wants us healthy. Holiness and health come from the same Anglo-Saxon root word. Holiness is to your soul what good health is to your body. When God purifies your heart, the disease of sin is removed, and you are truly healthy once again. When you allow God to make you pure, you'll discover that the Christian life is true joy and freedom. You'll finally be whole. You'll be sanctified "through and through." Holiness is the ultimate healthy lifestyle.

God can keep you blameless. This purity will keep you straight in this "crooked and depraved generation." He not only cleanses you but also keeps you clean. When you're sanctified wholly, the allure of this world will be strangled. Once you were a little fascinated by sin; now you'll be repulsed by it. Before, you didn't like that neighbor; now your pleasure is to serve him or her. You'll discover that living is easier. It isn't that the sanctified Christian has an easier life. The burdens are not lighter, but you will have a greater measure of grace and a greater spiritual power to bear the burdens of life.

He will keep you blameless. Paul didn't say you would perform perfectly; your motives will be perfect, but not your performance. It isn't that you are now *unable* to sin. It is that you are enabled *not* to sin. You may do wrong, but you won't do it intentionally. You may grieve God, but you won't do it deliberately. Your judgment will be flawed. You will make mistakes, but God will not blame you. He will consider you blameless.

It's true that God can make you pure and blameless, but there's no room for you to be boastful about it. A majority of people may be offended if you're always announcing, "I'm holy," or "I'm sanctified." That would sound as if you had really accomplished something. It would be better for you to testify like this: "God has graciously sanctified me." or "Through no merit of my own, God is making me holy." You see, the glory goes to the Sanctifier, not the sanctified.

Paul wrote, "So that you may become blameless and pure, children of God without fault in a crooked and depraved generation." Hundreds of generations have passed since he wrote those words, and each one has been more crooked and more depraved than the last one, right up until today, where we find ourselves living in a perverse generation. Sin is rampant. Temptation is oppressive. The selfishness and greed of today have never been equaled. People have never been more difficult to get along with. If there ever was a day that we needed sanctified laypersons, it's today. He can work in you if you'll surrender. This can be reality for you today. Won't you seek Him?

Roy's Story

My brother, Roy, by his own admission lived for the devil from the age of 18 to 48. As a boy, he sensed a call to ministry, but he ran from that call for all those years. He and his wife had two beautiful children. Roy was very successful in the insurance business, and for twenty-four years he had what he thought was a happy marriage.

However, the marriage collapsed, and with it his world collapsed. All of this drove him back to the Lord.

He said,

> I gave my life to Christ on December 27, 1988, and I resolved to serve Christ for the rest of my life. I gave up all the bad habits I had developed over the years and began studying the Word. I returned to the church of my childhood. I heard anointed Holiness preaching and soon realized that I was lacking this establishing grace. On July 13, 1989, I found myself unable to sleep. I was troubled and needed all that God could give me. It was a hot, sultry night in Dallas as I began to walk around the block in my neighborhood. I prayed in earnest, telling God what I needed. I needed Him to restore my marriage. I needed Him to fix my family. I needed Him to change my world.
>
> Finally, I realized that God was saying what I really needed was for me to be changed. I needed a deeper work inside me. So I finally prayed, *O God change me. Whatever you want me to do or be, I'll do it. Lord, I surrender all. Even if I have to walk around this block until my legs are stubs, I must have your blessing.*
>
> Immediately I felt His peace and began praising God for His touch. However, I had walked only about ten feet when I began to wonder, *How do I know?* I stopped on the sidewalk and began to weep—*I don't know. I don't know.* I walked on, praying and asking for assurance from the Holy Spirit.

Surrendering again, I said, *I must know!* Once again, I claimed the promise of the Holy Spirit's fullness and began thanking and praising God for His gift. But then again, after walking a few more steps, the same question returned: *How do I know?* I cried louder, *I don't. I don't. I must. I must!*

I walked on, resolved not to stop walking and praying that night until I knew that I knew. I took a few more steps, begging God for assurance. Suddenly, I stopped and looked down to my right. There in the perfectly mowed lawn was a single blade of grass standing up about two inches above all the other grass. I reached down, and through my tears I pulled that blade of grass out by the roots. I looked up into the clear, starry night and held that blade of grass up to the sky. I said, *Father, I'm no better that this blade of grass. I'm nothing!* At that moment, there came flowing over my head and running down my body a liquid warmth. It was an unmistakable divine moment. I knew that I knew that I knew. I bounced around the block enjoying sanctifying grace, praising and glorifying God.

Upon returning to the house that night, I opened my Bible, and this verse jumped off the page: "But if from there you seek the LORD your God, you will find him if you look for him with all your heart and with all your soul" (Deuteronomy 4:29). That blade of grass is still in my Bible today, marking that verse.

Roy's beautiful and dramatic testimony of entire sanctification will not be your testimony. God wants to do a similar work in your heart, but He'll tailor-make your experience. The details won't be the same, but the result will be the same. He'll make you pure and keep you blameless. Perhaps you're saying, "I've tried to be sanctified wholly, but I just can't seem to receive the blessing. I'm willing to pay the price, but it seems I never really by faith find this power in my life." If that's you, I wish I could meet you at the altar of your church or at your living room couch and kneel with you in prayer. It's so vitally important that you pray through on this.

In 1940 Nazarene General Superintendent J. B. Chapman wrote this beautiful prayer for entire sanctification. As he wrote it, he imagined kneeling with a person seeking entire sanctification. Perhaps as you read the prayer today, you could imagine that he's praying it just for you. Why don't you make it your prayer?

> *We come today, our Heavenly Father, to thank Thee for all the promises of mercy and grace which Thou hast made for us and for all men. We thank Thee for the blood of Jesus, which has been made an offering for us that we might come into Thy presence without fear. And we come today pleading that precious blood. We have no worth or merit of our own to bring—"simply to the cross we cling."*
>
> *We thank Thee for Thy Holy Spirit, who in answer to the blood has come to regenerate, to sanctify, to indwell*

and keep our hearts forevermore. There is no power on earth or in heaven that can reach and transform our hearts except Thy Holy Spirit. He alone is the executor of Thy will in the work of salvation, and we thank Thee for His presence and power that are available to us on terms that we are capable of meeting.

We thank Thee, O blessed Lord, for Thy Holy Word, the Bible, which Thou hast, through Thy Spirit and unsearchable providences, given to us to be our way bill and Guide Book. We thank Thee for the unfailing promises of this Book. We come pleading these today, as we seek special favors at Thy hand.

And now, O blessed Lord, we bring to Thee this, our dear brother and Thy child. We come to join with him in the prayer that Thou wilt this hour sanctify him and cleanse his heart from all sin and fill him with Thy perfect love. He has often prayed for this blessing. He believes this blessing is available to him, as to others who come seeking it with all their hearts. He feels his deep need of being thus sanctified and cleansed from sin. He is ready and willing this day to pay the price in full consecration, that his heart may be made wholly and forever Thine.

Come this day, O blessed Lord, and enable this Thy child to place himself with all his ransomed powers upon Thy altar for time and for eternity. Give him grace to part in spirit with every loved one on earth; as such parting may be necessary to go with Thee. Give him grace to separate himself from every fond ambition that he has ever felt or thought or known. Give him grace to place himself at Thy disposal without any shadow of reservation or any trace of reluctance. He cannot know the future or what it will bring forth, but give him grace to say a yes that will cover every question Thou mayest ever ask him from now on to the day when he shall see Thy face in heaven.

And as he comes with his unlimited gift, we pray Thee, pour out upon him Thy unlimited blessing. Thou hast ever challenged us to come with the promise that in such case Thou wilt not cast us out. Thou has challenged us to give our all to Thee that Thou mightest give Thine all to us and we claim that promise today. Ready and willing now for Thy worst, we come in faith to claim Thy best. Wilt Thou come just now and sanctify this Thy child? Sanctify him wholly. Sanctify him now. We trust Thee to do it.

Thy promise is like a platform on which we are required to step in order that the springs of holy water may flow forth for us. And now we step out upon that platform—Thy promise. We have believed Thou art able to do it. We have believed Thou art willing to do it. But now we believe Thou doest it. We take it at Thy hand. We receive it at Thy touch. We possess it in Thy Spirit. It is true even now!

Thanks be unto God for His unspeakable gift! The Comforter has come! "He fully saves me now!" Praise be unto the Triune God! Praise be to the Father who has willed this blessing to us! Praise be unto the Son who has worked the provisions for it! Praise be unto the Holy Spirit who has now come to witness in our hearts that the work is done! Praise be to God forevermore! Amen and amen.

6. Paul's CONTINUING TRANSFORMATION

. . . in which you shine as stars in the universe.

—Philippians 2:15

Paul was a former Golden Glove champion from Arkansas—a bigot, an alcoholic, and a perfect candidate for a life-changing encounter with Christ. He had a saintly mother who had prayed faithfully for him and his three siblings for years. Now she lay dying in the hospital, and Paul felt the wooing of the Holy Spirit to surrender to his mother's Christ. He knew his life was presently a frustrating struggle and that he needed the grace and peace his mother had.

He took his family to church that Sunday determined to go to the altar to pray. When the altar call was given, he made his way down. His wife, Barbara, followed. The three children, Paul Jr., Paula, and Phillip, followed too. He found the transforming power of Christ that morning. In those moments he was made a new creature in Christ Jesus. A light was ignited in his life, and he was determined to continue becoming what he had just been made.

But this light could not erase the memory of one of Paul Holderfield's darkest moments. Years before, while serving as a fireman in Little Rock, he was working out in front of the building when an African-American childhood friend named Jimmy came walking by. Jimmy had been kind to Paul and given him many rides to town. Jimmy stuck out his hand to shake. Paul, knowing that the other firemen were watching, rocked back and put his hands into his hip pockets, ignoring Jimmy's hand. He could tell by Jimmy's facial expression that he was very hurt. Paul went back into the firehouse and wept, because he knew he had mistreated his friend. This memory would prove to be life-altering for Paul.

After his conversion, Paul immersed himself in the church and soon began to bring children to Sunday School and church—some of them African-American. But even at church, this was met with some resistance. Paul felt God asking him to help start a church that would be open to all ethnic groups, so this faithful layman accepted the challenge. In 1971 he found an area in North Little Rock that the police had informed him had the worst crime rate in the state. It was the perfect place of darkness for Christ's light to shine.

Recently I was privileged to preach at this church, known as Friendly Chapel Church of the Nazarene. It's a growing church with varied ministries, among them a dynamic children's ministry, a soup kitchen and shelter, a gymnasium with sports outreach, lively church services, a housing rehab enterprise, and a thrift shop where everything is a dollar unless you don't have a dollar, and then it's free. That part of town has been revitalized by the light of Christ and the energy of a godly layperson who expended his life there and eventually became the pastor.

Not long ago I visited a rescue mission in Nashville. I didn't have a problem finding a parking place—the clients don't drive. With some embarrassment, I parked my nice car by the transportation the clients use—old yellow buses and rusty vans. I felt a little uncomfortable, because it seems I have so much and they have so little.

The men I met there were friendly and open. This shelter becomes their home for up to six months as they find help with their drug and alcohol addictions and seek a way back into productive society. I slipped into the doublewide mobile home that serves as the cafeteria and the chapel.

It was chapel time, and a young man named Joshua was preaching to about forty men. They all had their

Bibles open and were listening carefully. As I sat there on that rusty folding chair, my heart was moved. Joshua was talking about James 1:5, which says, "If any man lacks wisdom, he should ask God, who gives generously to all without finding fault, and it will be given to him." He told the men that God could give them wisdom in the choices they make. If they would just turn to Him, He would change them and their lives.

The men responded with a hope-filled, almost incredulous chorus of "Amen!"—as if to say, *Joshua, do you really mean it? Can God really change me and get me out of this mess?* Confidently, Joshua was saying, "Yes—my God can help you." I must tell you, those moments were precious to me. The presence of the Holy Spirit was so evident. The kingdom of God was there. The light was there.

When Matthew and Luke began their writings about Jesus, they did so chronologically. They spent much time writing about the birth of Jesus. However, Mark departed from this approach. He wanted to get to the main thing. Almost breathlessly, he raced through a few statements about John the Baptist and the baptism and temptation of Jesus. Then he said that Jesus went into Galilee and proclaimed, "The time has come. The kingdom of God is near. Repent and believe the good news!" (Mark 1:15). Have we read those words so much that we no longer hear them?

Similarly, in His charge to the newly gathered twelve apostles, Jesus said, "As you go, preach this message: 'The kingdom of heaven is near.' Heal the sick, raise the dead, cleanse those who have leprosy, drive out demons" (Matthew 10:7-8). This message is the first thing Jesus declared in His public ministry. It's also the first thing He told His disciples when He commissioned them. It must have been significant to Jesus. He mentions "the kingdom of God" or "the kingdom of heaven" eighty-six times in Scripture. He gave many parables to describe this kingdom. This concept filled His conversation.

Have we heard Jesus say that the Kingdom is near and thought He meant that *someday* the Kingdom would get here, that it was somewhere out in the future? I believe Jesus was actually saying that the Kingdom is at hand. It is near. In fact, it's already here. Jesus even said in Luke 17:21, "The kingdom of God is within you." The Kingdom is *here* just waiting for you and me to discover its true power and force.

We often hear people say, "We're building the kingdom of God." The fact is that we can't build it—but we *can* embrace it. We can't make it grow—but we *can* plant some seeds along the way. Our frustration comes when we get that confused. We begin worshiping our results rather than the King of the Kingdom. We begin talking a lot about "taking our church to the next level." We begin talking about what *we've* done to *make* the church grow. This only leads to our personal frustration.

In his book, *This Beautiful Mess: Practicing the Presence of the Kingdom of God,* Rick McKinley reminds us that as ministers and faithful laypersons, we're not manufacturers. We're farmers. Manufacturers construct things with their hands. They build. And anything you can build with your hands is still only a dead, inanimate object. Anything you can build becomes your kingdom, and in the end it only leads to frustration and death. Nothing you can build will live forever.

A better metaphor for us is farming. You're just a farmer. You take the precious seed of the Kingdom and drop it into the soil. Then you water it. You wait. You work. You weep. You weed. You wait some more. And then finally, if the soil is good, you may hear yourself whisper, "I think I see some fruit growing."

Farmers know that they didn't make that fruit grow. They just embraced the process. They added a little of their own efforts to the project and watched God make it happen.

God has blessed us with a great host of kingdom farmers. What does a kingdom person look like? How can we shine as stars in the universe?

Kingdom people don't live it up—they lay it down.

True kingdom people are not on a constant path of seeking pleasure and earthly happiness. They're laying down their lives in sacrificial surrender to God. They're also laying down seeds of service to God. Their deep, abiding joy is a result of being used by the Lord.

One of the brightest lights of the last century was a diminutive woman named Mother Teresa. She gave her life ministering to the poor and dying in Calcutta, India. While traveling to Darjeeling on the train in 1946, she felt God speaking to her. These moments gave direction to her life. The voice kept pleading with her, *Come, come, carry Me into the holes of the poor. Come be My light.* This became the theme of her life. In fact, "Come Be My Light" is the title of the book written by Brian Kolodiejchuk, which is a study of her private writings.

Ironically, Mother Teresa often felt darkness in her walk with Christ. Kolodiejchuk said, "The reality of her relationship with Jesus was truly a paradox. He was living in and through her without her being able to savor the sweetness of His presence. At prayer she would turn to Jesus and express her painful longing for Him. But it was only when she was with the poor that she perceived His presence vividly. There she felt Him to be so alive and so real."

As she ministered in hovels and heartbreak, she found the presence of Christ. She often exhorted her little band of followers to "find Jesus in the dark holes of the slums, in the most pitiful miseries of the poor." She tenderly cared for the dying and loved the poor. That moment on the train made her, but she spent years becoming what she was made there.

I'm thankful for the many Kingdom laypeople who have found true joy in laying down their lives in service to Christ.

Kingdom people don't sit back—they rise up.

People in the world who are not captivated by an eternal God-given purpose never know the joy of working with God to see His kingdom move forward. They tend to sit back and watch as the most powerful force in the universe just passes them by. But thankfully thousands of Kingdom people populate our churches. They're rising up in happy unison to experience God's kingdom all around them.

I was particularly moved by a *USA Today* article written by Tom Krattenmaker describing a powerful ministry in Portland, Oregon. Marshall Snider formed a group of volunteer Christians from many churches in Portland and called it "Bridgetown Ministries." They wear T-shirts bearing the words "Get out of the box." They've decided to get out of the church building and take their ministry to the streets. Every Friday night about one hundred homeless people gather under Burnside Bridge in downtown. About one hundred volunteers are there to meet them.

They set up a food kitchen, give haircuts, and pass out clothes. They even play some Jesus songs. Marshall's instruction to the workers is to look for Jesus in the face of the homeless. He often speaks about the "least of these" mentioned by Jesus in Matthew 25:40. There we are told that when we feed the hungry, give water to the thirsty, clothe the naked, and visit the sick and imprisoned, our ministry to the "least of these" is actually ministry to Jesus himself. Marshall says that if you look closely, you just might find Jesus' eyes in those faces.

I would love to see those four folding chairs. They set them up with four basins of warm water in front. There's a pad for the volunteer to kneel on, and one by one the homeless take their places in the chairs. The volunteers remove smelly, wet socks, wash the dirty feet, dry them lovingly, powder them, and put new dry socks onto each foot—all the while looking up to see if they might catch a glimpse of Jesus' face. This humbling work is beautiful to imagine as the volunteers shine as stars in the universe. This loving service will draw folks to the loving Christ we serve. So today we rejoice that Kingdom people don't sit back. They rise up and give themselves in happy service to the Lord.

Kingdom people don't die in place—they press forward.

Kingdom people are always dreaming of what the Kingdom could be. They don't just mark time and eventually die in place. They continue to press forward for Jesus. J. B. Chapman said, "The success of the kingdom of God among men does not absolutely require eloquent preachers, brilliant writers, or famous singers, though these may be of service as incidentals; but it does depend upon everyday Christians who walk by faith when they can no longer see, and who believe when they cannot feel; they may sometimes have to go slowly, but they never stop. Their burdens may compel them to slacken to a walk, but nothing can force them into a faint."

In other words, Kingdom people don't die in place—they press forward. They may not be charging full speed. The struggles may have slowed them a bit, but they keep going forward. Farmers sometimes face hard times, droughts, and meager harvests, but they keep on laying down the seed.

You may be a layperson reading this today and you're struggling. You say, "Bob, I've been trying to help the Lord grow our church, but we just haven't seen many results." Friend, why should this surprise you? In one of Jesus' parables about the Kingdom, He talked about the farmer sowing seed in different types of soil. Some seed fell on hard ground. Some fell among thorns and rocks. The seed sprouted but quickly died. Some fell on the path and was eaten up by birds, so it never took root at all. But some of the seed fell on good soil and sprouted to bring forth a great harvest. Kingdom farmers just keep pressing on because they never know what will happen to the seed. Once in a while it will germinate. As Chapman said, "Even if you have slowed to a walk, you must not faint." Kingdom people press on. The next seed you put down just may be the one!

One of our challenges is that most of the seed we're sowing is right inside the walls of the church. We ably preach that people can be saved and entirely sanctified, but too often our declaration is heard only by the walls of the sanctuary and the regular attendees who don't doubt the truth of our message. But the Kingdom of God was never meant to be bottled up or boxed up in a church building. The Kingdom was never meant to be confined to elaborate rituals and boring readings. At Pentecost, where was the Spirit released? In the Temple? No. The Temple, priests, and altars were all passed by. The Spirit was infused into the hearts of the people. Truly and in greater measure, the Kingdom had come.

If you read through the gospels, you'll discover that Jesus had many conversations with people. If you count those conversations, you'll discover about 122 of them. Do you know how many of those conversations happened inside the church building? Only eight. Jesus was faithful to attend the church of His day, but He talked about the Kingdom as He walked the dusty trails and visited with the hurting people. He interjected talk of the Kingdom of God into every encounter He had. Not all the soil he spread seed on was hospitable, but he pressed forward anyway. Doesn't that say something to you and me today? The Kingdom of God was meant to be shared at meals, at ball games, on street corners, and in ordinary conversations in the everydayness of our lives.

Here's how to start. Get some people from your church together, and ask yourselves these questions. Where in our community could we find hurting people? What are simple ways that we could bring the Kingdom of God to that place? It might be a homeless shelter where you could serve some meals. It might be an orphanage where you could just hold some babies and sing "Jesus Loves Me" to them. It might mean finding a cold homeless person and giving him or her a new blanket. But as you embrace that situation with the love of Jesus, the Kingdom of God will begin to take root in some hearts, and they just may grow into disciples of Jesus Christ.

You say, "But Bob, I'm not sure that will make my church grow." Please remember—you're not a manufacturer. Jesus said, "I will build my church." The only thing He asked you to build was a disciple. He said to you, "Go and make disciples, baptizing them in the name of the Father, Son, and Holy Spirit." I believe that if we changed our focus to finding hurting people and helping them develop as disciples, God would grow His Church. We can help Jesus make disciples through the simple conversations of our lives.

He wants us to declare to everyone who will listen, "The Kingdom of God is at hand. Repent of your wayward ways. Believe the gospel Jesus Christ." And if we will, amazing things will happen. The sick will be healed. The dead will be raised. Lepers will be cleansed, and demons will be cast out. You say, "Well, Bob, I haven't seen much of that lately." Friend, I want you to rejoice, because those very miracles are happening in churches every week, and you're a part of that. Sin-sick people are being healed. People who are dead in their trespasses and sins are being resurrected to new life. The demons of addictions and bad attitudes are being cast out of people's lives. Our Christ is at work and wants to work through you, my faithful layperson friend.

In the previous chapter we talked about the life-changing moment when a believer is entirely sanctified. Christ wants to make you "blameless and pure, children of God without fault in a crooked and depraved generation." But He has reasons for that. He doesn't just want to prepare you for heaven. He doesn't just want to make you holy. This hallowed blessing isn't just for you. Paul the apostle goes on to say, "in which you shine like stars in the universe." He wants to give you this deeper work so that you'll be able to shine His light into this dark world. He wants His Kingdom to be released into this hurting place. He needs you to do His work, because there are so many who are lost and alone and desperate for God. He made you holy to be Christ to this world. You must become what He made you to be!

I must tell you a little more about Paul Holderfield. In January 1998 he had a heart attack and went on home to his mother and his Jesus. That very day, Paul Jr. quit his job as a bread route salesman and took over for his dad. It seems that the anointing and calling of the father now rests on the son.

When I visited there, I was moved by the presence of the Lord. In that service about 500 people gathered, sixty percent African-American and forty percent white.

Worshiping together in that service was the widow of a former governor of Arkansas and several homeless people. There were many college-educated persons and also many mentally disabled folks. In fact, a Down's syndrome man serving as usher, with a friend following close behind him, served me with the offering plate. The place was full of love and happiness and blessing—a taste of what heaven will be like. But most of all the sanctuary was ablaze with the light of Christ. "Stars" were in abundance.

The Bible says that the world will know we are Christians by our love. The city of North Little Rock noticed. They renamed the street in front of Friendly Chapel. It's no longer Arkansas Avenue. It's now Brother Paul Drive.

Oh, layperson friend, please shut down your computer for a while, give your television a rest, and go out and find a hurting person. Embrace that person, love him or her, and you, too, will sense that the Kingdom of God is near. There among the people you will find true joy and fulfillment. I know you may be afraid that if you love someone in Jesus' name they may ask you questions you won't know how to answer. But just relax—we're not here to win arguments, just people. There's power in the Kingdom of God. We just need to be out among the hurting so that His power and light in us can impact them.

Kingdom people don't live it up—they lay it down.
Kingdom people don't sit back—they rise up.

Kingdom people don't die in place—they press forward.

Did you notice the descent of the people who are *not* Kingdom people? They live it up, they sit back, and they die in place. They move from fun and hilarity to misery. But in stark contrast is the *ascent* of Kingdom people. They lay it down. They lay down their lives in humble sacrifice and service. They rise up, and they press forward. There's inexpressible pleasure and peace in their knowing they have been used by God to bless the Kingdom. Yes, the Kingdom of God is here. Can you see it? More important, will you share it?

7. Toni's POURED-OUT LIFE

I am being poured out like a drink offering on the sacrifice and service coming from your faith.

—Philippians 2:17.

Jack Welch, former CEO of General Electric, and Jane Welch, his wife of ten years, went through a difficult divorce. In the proceedings, her lawyer listed her known monthly expenses and suggested that this was the bare minimum need. Among many things, he mentioned $7,500 a month for her financial manager, $7,500 for clothes, $2,500 for dining out, $3,100 for gifts (how can I get on her list?), $10,360 for jewelry, and $20,000 for travel. The lawyer said she "needed at least $126,820 a month to survive." She *needed* this, even though she had $9 million in a Merrill Lynch account and $205,000 in her checking account. An interesting question to contemplate is—When is your *need* surpassed, and when does your *hoarding* begin?

The apostle Paul determined that his life would not be a collection but an offering. He spoke to the beautiful Christians in the church in Philippi and wrote in Philippians 2:17, "I am being poured out like a drink offering on the sacrifice and service coming from your faith." He was alluding to an Old Testament practice of pouring out a cup of wine with an animal sacrifice (Numbers 15). He was saying that these faithful laypeople had lived their lives in sacrifice and service, they had poured out their lives, and he has tried to do the same. The life of pouring is much different than the life of hoarding. In fact, they are antonyms.

Ironically, Paul learned the poured-out life from a layperson. The story is found in Acts 9:10-19. There we read that in Damascus, Ananias received a call from the Lord one day. In the vision God said, "Ananias," and immediately Ananias said, "Here I am, Lord." Ananias must have been spending a lot of time with the Lord, because he recognized His voice immediately. All God said was Ananias's name, and Ananias knew that it was God. God gave him definite directions, telling him to go find Saul. He explained that he would find him on Straight Street and that Saul would be unable to see when he (Ananias) got there.

At first Ananias argued with God. After all, this Saul was a dangerous man! He had been persecuting the Christians in Jerusalem, and now he had the authority to do the same thing in Damascus. Ananias knew that he was probably at the top of Saul's list, since his name began with "A." But Ananias decided that he would obey God—even if it meant that he might die. He would do what God wanted him to do. Ananias was willing to pour out his life in service to God. So he went.

When he arrived, he entered the house and said, "Brother Saul. . ." (verse 17). Isn't that beautiful? He could have entered that house with fear and suspicion, knowing what Saul had done to some of his Christian friends—but instead he said, "Brother Saul, the Lord—Jesus, who appeared to you on the road as you were coming here—has sent me so that you may see again and be filled with the Holy Spirit." That day, through the ministry of Ananias and the power of the Holy Spirit, Saul became Paul, a great missionary and author of half of the New Testament. The poured-out life that he later wrote about was taught to him by a faithful layman.

This is the poured-out life. Risk your own personal safety and comfort and go to the blind men and women around you who need their spiritual sight restored. There are many around you who are blind to the beauty of serving Jesus. They have no comprehension that Jesus can live in and through them. Their human nature is to hoard the stuff of life—they are truly blind.

A few years ago, Carol and I attended my high school reunion in Beatrice, Nebraska. It was exciting to see old friends. We found out who had the most children, who was bald, and who had gained the most weight. It's amazing what a few years will do to a person. One man who had always hated school had earned his Ph.D. in human development. I guess he developed. They asked me to pray the invocation at the banquet. Not wanting to pass up the opportunity, I slipped in a little preaching in the prayer.

Carol and I sat at the head table with the master of ceremonies. John had been a leader and a sports star. During the meal, he told me about what had happened in his life. He had married one of the popular girls at school. He and Susan had divorced after a number years because they had "been going in different directions." He spoke of it so nonchalantly, as if it really wasn't a big deal. But then later in the conversation, he asked me what I told couples thinking of divorce, and I was able to share with him for a few minutes. He finally admitted that down deep, he ached. Life hadn't been that great to him, and he was honest enough to quietly admit it to me. I noticed that he smiled a lot that night, but it was just with his mouth. His eyes and his heart didn't seem to be smiling.

As I looked out at those two hundred fifty faces, I realized that many of them seemed to be smiling just like John. They had blind, hollow eyes and empty faces. As Carol and I drove back to my parents' home that night, we talked about our feelings. I must tell you—it was rather depressing. I had seen a great many people reaching for things they thought would bring happiness and satisfaction. They were reaching in the wrong direction.

But do you know what bothered me most about the evening? It was not them, but me. I was a little disturbed by what I had seen, but I wasn't all that concerned. What bothered me was that I was not more bothered. I found myself praying, *O God, fill me with more love and concern for lost people who don't know Christ. O Lord, how can I be so unmoved by all this? Give me a vision of you weeping over Jerusalem. Give me a vision of blind people with empty faces and empty hearts. Give me a vision of people suffering an eternity in hell. O God—make me more concerned.*

Empty faces bother people who live poured-out lives. They weep for lost men and women. They sometimes lose sleep and agonize over a loved one or neighbor who doesn't know Christ. They're constantly on the lookout for empty faces and blind eyes. They get great pleasure in being able to help them and point them to Jesus Christ. They're willing to be inconvenienced just for the opportunity to tell someone about the Lord.

Paul learned the poured-out life from a layman. So have I. It's been my privilege to pastor and work with many wonderfully dedicated laypersons through the years. They somehow discovered that it wasn't just the pastor's responsibility to see people come to Jesus. They've been involved in ministry. It was their driving force. They just wanted to help. They wanted their lives to make a difference.

Toni

I've known Toni Powers for more than thirty-five years. She's my mother-in-law, and you'll read no mother-in-law jokes here. She's a wonderful woman of God. As long as I've known her, she's lived the poured-out life. I've often heard her say, "I love to talk to people about the Lord." Until she was eighty years old, she worked hard cleaning homes and offices. For her, one of the most important reasons for doing this was so that she would have opportunities to witness for Christ.

When she began cleaning for a new client, she looked to see if there were any religious pictures or Bibles around. If she found any, it was an opportunity to start a conversation. She says most people want to hear about the Lord, and many of her clients have gone to church with her. She prayed with many of them, and some of them found the Lord. This is the great pleasure of her life.

A few years ago she began cleaning a doctor's home. The doctor and his wife were in their fifties, and Toni noticed there was nothing in the home that would indicate they were people of faith. One day she brought up the Lord in conversation with the lady. The lady became very cold and said, "We're Catholics." Toni could tell they just weren't interested, but she kept praying for them and looking for another opportunity.

Sometime later they returned from a ski trip in Colorado, and Toni noticed that the lady was limping. Toni asked, "Did you fall skiing?"

The lady said, "No, I didn't fall, Toni. It's worse than that. I've been diagnosed with an inoperable brain tumor, and I don't have long to live." Toni replied that she would be praying for her. The lady said, "Toni, I really appreciate that."

Toni went home that day rejoicing because the coldness was gone, and she knew she would soon have an opportunity to talk with her about the Lord.

The next time she came to clean, Toni gave the lady a book about the Lord. She explained that she could know Jesus and be confident that when she died she would go to heaven. The lady was happy to hear it. She started asking questions, and finally she said, "I do want to go to heaven when I die."

Toni prayed with the lady that day, and she gave her life to Jesus. Three months later she died, and Toni was so thankful that God had given her the ministry of cleaning houses. Pouring out and cleaning up are a terrific combination.

Margaret

I've known Margaret for more than fifty years, and I can testify without reservation that she is a laywoman who has lived the poured-out life. She's my mother, and the greatest joy of her life, when she was able, was helping people. When I was a youngster, we lived only three blocks from the church, but every Sunday morning we left the house an hour before Sunday School began. I sat in the back seat, and we would drive all the way across town in the opposite direction of the church and pull up in front of a little ramshackle house. Dad and I would wait in the car, and Mom would make her way down the long sidewalk to the Summervilles' front porch. She would knock and then just march right in. I guess she had permission. She knew where the four children slept, and she would wake them up and wash their faces and get them dressed. Then, like the Pied Piper, she would lead them out to the car, and every Sunday I had to share the back seat with the Summerville kids. Then, after Sunday School and church, we would take them back home again.

I always hated this, but Mom seemed to love it. I guess she decided that if the Summervilles had a chance of making it to heaven, it just might be because she was willing to be inconvenienced. She was willing to take her time, use her gasoline, and give her love just so they could hear about Jesus. I learned the poured-out life from watching my mother.

If you visited our little church on Sunday morning, you were invited to come to our house for lunch. My mother knew all the recipes you could stretch by adding water, depending on how many people came home with us. For instance, you can add water to chicken and noodles, and it will feed many more visitors. She knew all those tricks. We didn't have to have fancy food. We just had to have loving food. Folks would love to visit our home because of my mother's love and hospitality. Margaret loved the ministry that God had given her. It was the ministry of the kitchen. Pouring out and cooking up are a terrific combination.

Gertrude

Gertrude was a special lady in my life. She lived her nine decades in poured-out ministry. As mentioned earlier in this book, she was my speech teacher when I was in college, and Carol and I stayed in contact with her after that. In her later years her activities were greatly limited, but she still had a ministry.

A few years ago she told me about her ministry of shopping. She would go to the mall or the grocery store, and since her vision was limited, she couldn't read the price tags. So she would just stop people and say, "Would you please read this price for me?" I don't know too many people who could resist a frail, white-haired lady who asked that. Gertrude said that half of them would take her all over the store, helping her, and while they were walking, she would witness to them.

She didn't need some of the stuff she was buying, but she was having great fun telling people about Jesus. Many of them would begin to tell their problems to this sweet old lady in the store, and she would happily pray for them. Some she led to Christ. She said to me, "Remember: with God all things are possible." Gertrude discovered the ministry of shopping. Pouring out and buying up are a terrific combination.

It happened in a little eastern Wyoming town. It was lunchtime, and the mother walked to the front porch to call little four-year-old Janie to come in and eat. But Janie wasn't there. She wasn't in the front yard. The mother walked around the house, but Janie wasn't in the backyard either. Her mother's intuition was beginning to work, and she had the strange feeling that her little girl was lost. Janie had never been gone like this before. She always stayed in the yard.

The mother remembered the busy highway running right in front of the house. Could it be? Could someone have stolen her little girl? They could be miles away by now. Her little girl was lost, and she was almost beside herself. She called the neighbors. She called her husband at work. She called the local police and the state police. She called all her little girl's friends, asking, "Is my Janie there?"

Soon it was announced on the radio. The whole city was looking for the lost little girl. Lunchtime didn't matter. Work schedules didn't matter. Afternoon appointments didn't matter. Absolutely nothing mattered but finding that lost child.

I pray that you and I will adopt that kind of attitude regarding lost people in this world. May the Lord give us a burden for people with empty faces and blind eyes. There are lost people out there, and I believe He can help us care so much that nothing else will matter but finding them for Jesus. Lunch won't matter. Work schedules and afternoon appointments won't matter. *O Lord, give us that kind of concern.*

By the way, they found Janie. She had crawled under the front porch to escape the hot Wyoming sun and had fallen asleep. There are lost people today not far from your front porch. They're not far from your desk at work. There are lost people with empty faces and blind eyes everywhere, and may God help us to find them. This is the heart cry of every great layperson I've met.

Gertrude spent her last few months in a nursing home in Oklahoma. Carol talked to her one day, and she was uncharacteristically flustered. She asked Carol to pray for her. She had noticed that some of her special possessions were being taken from the room. She thought that someone was stealing from her, and she wanted God to help her. So Carol and I just simply prayed for her.

About a month later, Carol called her back to check on her. Immediately Gertrude started telling her, "Carol, God told me that I wasn't supposed to worry about those things, because I wasn't going to be able to take those things where I was going anyway." Then she said, "God told me that He had a job for me here in the nursing home. He said, 'I want you to love Dorothy for me.' So the next time they came to take me to the dining room, I told the aide to put me over there at Dorothy's table. The aide said, 'You don't want to sit by Dorothy. Nobody likes to sit with her. She yells and screams all the time.' But I said, 'Yes, that's where I want to sit. And Carol, I've been sitting with Dorothy now for a couple of weeks, and Carol—Dorothy isn't screaming anymore."

That's the last time we spoke with Gertrude. She lived her life to the very end, not hoarding but being poured out as a love offering to God. That's the way I want to go. Don't you?

8. *Ollie's* GREAT GREETINGS

Press on. —Philippians 3:14
Eagerly await. —Philippians 3:20
Stand firm. —Philippians 4:1

In the right place and at the right time, every Sunday morning you would find Ollie greeting folks in the church lobby. For many years Ollie served his church in this capacity. Toward the end of this service, you would find him with an oxygen tank around his shoulder, and because of his poor eyesight, he probably wouldn't recognize you until he heard your voice. But Ollie would be there if he possibly could make it. He would be quick to give you a hug and thank you for coming. He would be positive about what a great service we were going to have that day, and he would let you know that you were going to love being there. As long as God gave him strength, Ollie was there—in the right place at the right time.

There was a time over sixty-eight years ago, however, when Ollie was in the wrong place at the wrong time. On December 7, 1941, he was on Wake Island as the Japanese planes flew over on their way to bomb Pearl Harbor. He was there not as one of the many Marines but as a civilian working for Morrison-Knudsen. Two hundred dollars a month was much more that he could earn back home in Paris, Illinois. On December 8 the Japanese planes attacked Wake Island, and Ollie took a bullet in his left arm. He knew then that he was in the wrong place at the wrong time.

It was to get much worse.

By December 22 forty Japanese ships had surrounded the island, and the commander decided to surrender. Ollie and a Marine climbed to the top of the dugout and hung a white sheet on the flagpole. Soon the Japanese soldiers were rounding up the Americans and gathering them at the airstrip. They took all their rings, watches, and coins and stripped them naked. They threw the paper money away, because they believed they would soon take over the United States and that our country's paper money would be worthless.

When the entire island had been secured, the Japanese soldiers set up machine guns aimed at the Americans. The American commander approached the Japanese commander and asked what their intentions were. The Japanese soldier explained that his orders were to take no prisoners, so he was going to kill them. Ollie's commander requested that the Japanese commander wire Tokyo and ask that his orders be rescinded.

The Japanese commander agreed to this request, but the machine guns stayed in place. Ollie and his comrades sat for two days without food, water, or clothing. Late Christmas day the orders came that the Americans were to be taken prisoner, and they were returned to their barracks.

Thus began Ollie's life in prisoner-of-war camps. It was horrible, unspeakable, inhumane treatment. Ollie was taken to China and Japan to work in slave labor. Many of his friends were killed, beheaded, or beaten to death if they couldn't work. He lived in a two-by-six-foot space. He was given some blankets, a pillow filled with sawdust, a canvas pillowslip, a bowl with chopsticks, and a cup. A meal consisted of a cup of barley and soybeans cooked together and a cup of green tea.

It was four months before Ollie was allowed to take a bath—if you could call it that. The Japanese filled a large vat with water and started a fire under it. Eighteen hundred men took a bath that day in the same water. Ollie said the water was pretty thick by the time the last man went through.

One day Ollie was able to receive a large ball of rice from another man. He was going to hide in the latrine and eat it, but a Japanese soldier stopped him and searched him. He took the rice ball away and made Ollie stand at attention while he tied knots in the end of a rope. Then he stood back and struck Ollie repeatedly so the rope would rap around his face. Then he would give the rope a jerk. The soldier did this until he was tired. As a result of that beating, Ollie was legally blind. Ollie knew that if he resisted, he would have been killed.

The Japanese soldiers had standing orders to kill all prisoners of war the minute American troops set foot on Japan. Ollie believed that the atomic bomb dropped on Japan saved his life, because it brought a quick end to the war. American soldiers liberated his camp after three years and eight months of torture. Ollie then weighed just 125 pounds.

Ollie said, "I could not have gone through the ordeal on my own. Many times when I was ready to give up, God carried me through." It's the Lord who carries us through. Your disappointments and difficulties may not be quite as dramatic as Ollie's, but your struggles are no less real and challenging. You know, as Ollie knew, that without Christ you can't keep going. The apostle Paul knew the trials and struggles that every layperson faces, so he gave three short greetings or encouraging words: "Press on," "Eagerly await," and "Stand firm."

Press On

In the prisoner-of-war camp, if you didn't press on, you didn't survive. Ollie said that he had seen many men who could have made it, but they just gave up, lay down, and soon died. Paul knew this also, so he challenged the saints in Philippi to forget about the past and strain toward the future. He said, "I press on toward the goal to win the prize" (Philippians 3:14).

I've talked to many laypersons who want to focus on past hurts and disappointments. They seem to be stymied by the prospect of continuing on. They look for opportunities to hang up their spiritual uniforms and retire from active Christian service. But I don't think that's what Paul had in mind for us. He said, "Press on." I agree. Don't quit—keep going. There are people who need you. There are young Christians watching you. Your children can see if you really live what you've preached to them. Guard your influence. You must press on!

In one of our church building projects I installed some rolls of fiberglass insulation. I did not wear goggles on the job and learned a painful lesson after getting some fiberglass in my left eye. I knew something was in there, but I couldn't see it. I couldn't sleep that night, because it felt as if there was a little green man with a pitchfork under my eyelid. Every time I blinked, he jabbed me.

I went to the doctor the next morning. He found four microscopic pieces of fiberglass imbedded in my eyelid and scratching my eyeball, so he extracted them. On Wednesday he found two more. On Thursday he found another one, and he said that if it was still bothering me on Friday, I would have to go to the operating room, where he could use a bigger microscope. That didn't sound too wonderful to me, so on Friday I was miraculously healed.

I was amazed that such small things could make my whole body miserable. I couldn't even see them when the doctor took them out of my eye, but each time he removed one, I felt better. They may have appeared to be small and insignificant, but when they were someplace, you knew it.

Laypeople are like that. I don't mean that they're causing pain and tears, although I suppose some are like that. What I mean is that some laypeople may think they're small and insignificant, but when they're around, they make their presence known. They're making a positive contribution to the life of the church. You know when they're there, and you certainly know when they're not there. They probably don't realize it, but their influence is great.

I think of a beautiful, stately, ninety-year-old woman in Tampa named Rebecca. She had lost her husband and several of her children, yet she continued to press on. She was an influencer at church—smiling, positive, encouraging to her pastor, uplifting to everyone around her. I think of Moe and Shirley in Colorado. Even after losing their successful business, they pressed on, never mad at God, just happy to be able to serve Him. I think of Willis in Denver, who for years cared for his invalid and homebound wife, never complaining and always faithful to the church he loved.

Perhaps life hasn't been perfect for you, and you've had more than your share of disappointments. But remember that your influence is great. People are watching. Be sure to press on.

Eagerly Await

If you met Ollie at the church door, he might greet you with Paul's words in Philippians 3:20: "Eagerly await a Savior." Ollie said that one of the ways he survived was that he always believed the war could not last more than six months. God would somehow intervene, and he would be home before six months had passed. He carried that belief through the whole war. He was eagerly awaiting God's intervention.

Laypeople need to adopt that kind of thinking today. Jesus will help us through. This problem at church that seems so big, so impossible to solve, will be worked out by the Lord. It's His church. He's in control. He'll come.

You know what we do, though. We take things into our own hands and begin to manipulate and plan and coerce. I received a call from a layman friend of mine one day. I was his district superintendent, and he needed to meet with me. I asked him what the conversation would be about so that I could be thinking and praying about it. He mentioned some troubles that his church had experienced four years earlier. I said to myself, *I thought that was over. It's done. We can't fix it now. I wonder why he still needs to speak about it.* I must tell you that I dreaded that meeting—I'm happy to tell you that I was very wrong.

We met for lunch, and I was nervous during the small talk. Then he started in. "Dr. Bob, do you remember that trouble we had at the church? I need to ask forgiveness."

He had my full attention then. "I was disloyal to my pastor. I helped organize some meetings, and we talked about our pastor and our differences of opinion with him. We didn't like the way he was doing things. We didn't like his attitude. We wrote letters to you and to the General Superintendents."

By this time my friend was crying, and I was crying. He continued: "I've felt bad about this for four years, and I need some peace. We should have just waited on God to come and solve the problem. I was wondering if you would call that pastor and ask if he'll talk to me. I'll drive to the state where he now pastors. I'll do anything to ask his forgiveness. There are some other people in the church who left whom I offended. Would you call them to see if they'll let me meet with them?" My layman friend was willing to do whatever he could to try to make amends. He did follow through.

I'll never forget that meeting and will forever admire my friend. In my estimation, he's a wonderful layman. He learned a valuable truth: there are times when you just need to "eagerly await" the Savior.

Stand Firm

The apostle Paul wrote, "My brothers, you whom I love and long for, my joy and crown, that is how you should stand firm in the Lord, dear friends" (Philippians 4:1). Ollie made it through his ordeal because he didn't waver. He was a good plodder. He just kept going. He stood firm in the Lord.

Sometimes laypeople begin to sense that their commitment is beginning to waver. There are times we need to reevaluate our level of commitment and with David declare, "My heart is steadfast [fixed], O God, my heart is steadfast" (Psalm 57:7).

You can't overestimate the importance of reestablishing your determination to be committed. Dean Kelley wrote, "When a handful of wholly committed human beings give themselves fully to a great cause or faith, they are virtually irresistible. They cut through the partial and fleeting commitments of the rest of society like a buzz saw through peanut brittle."

When I pastored in Hutchinson, Kansas, a successful businessman named Don attended our church. He and Sharron would sometimes take Carol and me to dinner. Don would always introduce me not as "a pastor" but by saying, "This is my pastor." He always seemed to emphasize *my* as if he were proud that I was his pastor. I felt honored by his kindness. Whenever I think about "standing firm in the Lord," I think about Don. His father was a grand Christian. And when his father died,

Don wanted to honor him and his faithfulness to Jesus at the funeral. So he wore a pair of his dad's shoes to the funeral. They didn't really match Don's beautiful suit, and the shoes were pretty scuffed, but it was Don's way of saying, "My dad stood in these shoes, and I'm proud to do so also. He followed in the footsteps of Jesus, and that's my plan too. I, with my father, will stand firm in the Lord!" I never forgot that story, and when my dad died, I did what Don did: I wore my dad's shoes to the funeral.

I want to urge you to stay true to Jesus. Sometimes you may get frustrated with the way things are going or not going at the church, but please stand firm in the Lord. I know that often you're not appreciated for your labors at the church, but just keep going. Perhaps it's been a long time since someone said, "Thanks," or "We really are thankful for you," but don't worry about that.

O Lord, help us to be willing to stand firm for you, whatever you ask of us.

When I think of the vast majority of the laypeople in the Church today, I'm thankful that they're faithful. They're not in the limelight, but they sure are the lights of their worlds. They'll probably always be anonymous, but someday they'll be first in line. Dear layperson, bring these beautiful greetings to your world. Press on! Eagerly await! Stand firm! There are many prisoners out there who need the news.

9. Larry's GRACIOUS GIVING

Not one church shared with me in the matter of giving and receiving, except you only. . . . Not that I am looking for a gift, but I am looking for what may be credited to your account. . . The gifts you sent . . . are a fragrant offering, an acceptable sacrifice, pleasing to God.

—Philippians 4:15, 17-18

For twenty-five years I had an established, very unpopular rule at our house: no pets! I'm embarrassed to tell you—I got soft. I had all kinds of reasons for the rule. Pets were dirty. They got in your way. When you left the house on vacation, you either had to put them in the kennel or take them with you. We lived in the church parsonage, and the board wouldn't approve pets. At least that's what I claimed. The greatest reason was that pets made you spend a lot of money with very little in return.

Carol and the kids just didn't buy it.

Then one day, fate, nature, Carol, and the kids all ganged up on me. A stray cat was scratching at our back door. It looked hungry, sad, weather-beaten, and pregnant. Carol told me that she hadn't been feeding the poor thing, but I have my doubts. It was February, and Carol said she could feel the kittens moving in the mother. I wasn't thrilled to hear that bit of obstetrical news. Then Carol explained that the poor mother needed some sort of delivery room. I explained that God had taken care of her this long and that He could continue without our assistance. She placed a cardboard box on the back deck, and we left for the day. When we returned, the neighborhood animal population had increased by four. Carol thought they were sooo cute. I thought they looked like scrawny little mice.

I reminded Carol of the standing twenty-five-year house rule. She said she would find nice homes for them. She quickly found homes for three of the kittens, but one kitten was anti-social and slower than the rest. No one seemed to want him. By this time, my grown kids were ganging up on me, and Carol was looking longingly at this cat that nobody wanted, and I did a dumb thing. It was a moment of weakness. I don't know what came over me. I suggested a name. Now the cat was yellow and white and Carol didn't think that "Smokey" fit. Smokey was a name you gave a gray cat, but she wasn't suggesting anything else. She said, "Oh, I love that name. Let's call him 'Smokey.'" A smarter man would have known that he had just made a big mistake.

Smokey grew on me. I didn't let anybody know that, of course. I was always complaining about finding hair on my dark suits. Fortunately, he was not the kind of cat that would jump up on you, so it wasn't a big problem. Once in a while, when no one was looking, I would reach down to pet Smokey. If Carol entered the room while I was doing this, I would say something like "You dumb cat. Stop rubbing up against me."

Smokey had been a part of our home for five years when Carol decided that it wasn't fair to him. Our schedule required us to be gone from home a lot, and we would have to put him in the kennel where he would live in a small cage for twenty-four hours a day. She announced one day that she had decided to give him away. I immediately said, "Great! It's about time. I've been spending a lot of money on that cat." Inside I was thinking, *What? You can't give my Smokey away! He's given me a lot of joy. It's been fun to watch him and talk to him.* She made a lot of calls and found that the humane society would take him and find him a good home.

She wanted me to go with her to take him. I couldn't. I was conveniently busy. When she got there, she placed the cage with Smokey and his food and his toys onto the counter. She was expecting the man to ask what kind of cat he was and if he was good with children and things like that. But he was in a hurry. He did ask, "Are you going to give a donation?" Carol replied, "Yes, fifty dollars," thinking that a generous donation may help in finding Smokey a good home. She left crying and arrived home crying. I'm glad I wasn't there. I would have been blubbering too.

The next morning I awoke to see Smokey staring at me. Carol had his photograph on the dresser. I begged her to put it away, but she refused. She can be cruel at times. I said, "Carol, did you sleep very well?"

She responded, "No, did you?"

"Well, I hate to admit it," I replied, "but all I saw was Smokey in an ugly cage with that cute little face of his, looking out through those bars wondering when we were coming to get him. But they did say that they would find him a good home, didn't they?"

That morning we were scheduled to be at a meeting, so we went. Carol was talking to a lady and telling her the story of taking Smokey to the humane society. The lady said, "You do know, don't you, Carol?—they kill the pets if no one adopts them within a week." Carol was shocked and told me what the lady said.

I'm a little embarrassed to tell you this, but we were at the humane society within the hour. The building was an ugly warehouse on the wrong side of town. I couldn't go in—I was too chicken. I waited in the car. Brave Carol went in and with almost panic in her voice asked, "Is Smokey still here?" The employee checked—and he was. Then the employee said, "That will be forty dollars for one night's room and board and the paperwork to adopt him back."

The reunion was wonderful. As we drove down the street, we let Smokey out of his cage. We were on our way to a funeral, and I had a dark gray suit on. Smokey found his way to my lap, and by the time we got to the funeral, I had hair all over me. I didn't mind—Smokey was back.

My biggest reason for not having a pet was that they cost a lot of money for very little in return. Now that I've known Smokey, I see it differently. He did cost me a lot of money, but I received a lot from him. The pleasure of his companionship meant a great deal. Somehow, you get attached. Giving and receiving are like that. You give. You receive. Then you give some more. You feel good in the giving, and you're blessed in the receiving.

Paul felt that way about the faithful laypersons in the Philippian church. He ended his letter talking about their generosity. He explained that they shared with him in the matter of giving and receiving and suggested that as they gave to him, God was noting their generosity and that He was crediting fruit to their account. Their gifts to Paul were a fragrant offering and sacrifice that God really appreciated. They were not giving to Paul because they planned on receiving something in return. They were not giving to Paul because they felt compelled to build up their account with God. Because they loved, they just had an inner compunction to give. They wanted to give. They couldn't help but give. This beautifully describes great laypersons. Most every pastor has been blessed by gracious givers in the church, and the givers have been blessed by the giving.

It has been my happy privilege to pastor many wonderful givers. Some of them were wealthy. Some of them were poor. Most of them were somewhere in the middle. Whether or not you're a gracious giver has little to do with your financial net worth.

One lady I pastored in Colorado was named Virgie. She had little of this world's goods. After Virgie experienced a massive stroke, one side of her body did not work well. Yet for years you could see her limping along the roadside picking up cans to sell for missions. She was a gracious giver.

I have a dear friend in Hutchinson, Kansas, named Larry. Larry is a gracious giver. He has spent his life giving. When I was his pastor, he had a successful meat business in which he employed four hundred people. He was a wealthy man. Few men have been his equal in generosity. He learned generosity from his father, Frank. When they needed a new building for the church in Pratt, Frank refused to build himself a new house until generously giving toward the construction of the new church.

Larry lived with his family in a simple three-bedroom ranch house and gave large sums of money so that the new church could be built in Hutchinson. He wanted that church to be the best it could be. Along with the many other faithful laypersons of that congregation, an extraordinary worship facility was built to the glory of God. Then once the church was built, just like his father before him, Larry felt comfortable to build his own dream house. The Lord came first.

Gracious givers are often unpretentious people. One Sunday night I noticed Larry had on bowling shoes when he came to church. I had never seen bowling shoes worn with a nice business suit. I pointed out Larry's stylish Sunday footwear. "Aren't those bowling shoes, Larry?" I said.

"Well, yes," he said. "I'm never going to wear them out bowling. I might as well wear them to church."

Larry has always been burdened for lost people. I've seen him weep over his neighbor who didn't know the Lord, wondering how he could reach him for Jesus. One Sunday morning on his way to church, Larry saw an older couple standing by their car looking at a flat tire. He stopped and offered to help. Larry took off his suit coat and changed the tire. When he finished, he asked, "What are you folks doing today?"

They said, "Oh, we're just out for a Sunday drive."

Larry saw his opening. "Well, I'm on my way to church. You would love our church. Why don't you follow me?" Well, what could they say to this kind man with mud all over his bowling shoes after he had just changed their flat tire? They followed him to church. Soon they were at the altar finding Jesus. Soon afterward they joined the church. It happened because a gracious giver was willing to help and invite.

At Christmastime, Larry would bring me a bunch of gifts with a list of names. He would explain that these were the people he had been working on. They needed the Lord, and he thought that if I would deliver the gifts, I might have a chance to pray with some of them. He told me that I could just tell them the gifts came from the church. He didn't want any credit. He just wanted somebody to find Jesus. Laymen like Larry are a "fragrant offering" to pastors.

I love gracious givers like my sister, Anita, and her husband, Ron. When Mom and Dad weren't able to live by themselves anymore, Ron and Anita took them into their home. They have taken seriously the words "Honour thy father and thy mother" (Exodus 20:12, KJV) and truly lived them out in their lives. They tenderly cared for Dad until he went home to be with the Lord. Now that Mom is in the nursing home, Anita checks on her every day and lovingly takes care of a myriad of details. I'm sure God is crediting this to their account.

I love gracious givers like my dad. He was not a wealthy man. He was a printer at the local newspaper and typed on a linotype machine for fifty years. The most he ever made in one year was $8,000. He was the church treasurer, and it was his responsibility to give the pastor his check every Sunday morning. There were some Sundays when there just wasn't enough in the church account to pay the pastor. Dad would take money out of his personal account and put it into the church account so he would have enough to pay the preacher. My dad was one of the thousands of humble, quiet, gracious givers in the Church. I'm proud of my heritage.

My dad didn't give because he thought he was going to get something in return. He gave because he loved the Lord. If you had visited my dad in his room at the nursing home before he died, you might have thought that God had not blessed him very much. Anita fixed up his room very nicely, but there's only so much you can do with half a room. He shared the room with a man named Ed. Dad had a borrowed bed and chair. There was a skinny table with wheels that hung over his bed. There was his ever-present wheelchair there. On the wall you would have found a clock, a red bird that he painted in craft class, some pictures of his family, a corkboard with a few greeting cards thumb-tacked on it, and a calendar on which my mother dutifully crossed out the days as they passed. In the little closet were a few pairs of pajamas and some jigsaw puzzles. And that was my father's total existence.

Are you tempted to say that God had forsaken him? Don't be. I never heard my Dad complain. After he was there about a week, he asked my mom when she was going to take him home. She explained to him through an abundance of tears that she just couldn't lift him anymore and that he required around-the-clock help.

He never asked her again and began calling the nursing home "my hotel." He was satisfied—satisfied in Jesus. He knew that a man's life does not consist in the abundance of things (Luke 12:15). Through the years he had given much, and he had received much. God had been faithful.

Paul ends his conversation about giving with one of the most beautiful promises in the Bible. In Philippians 4:19-20 he writes, "My God will meet all your needs according to his glorious riches in Christ Jesus. To our God and Father be glory forever and ever. Amen." I'm certain that Virgie and Larry and Anita and Dad and Smokey would agree. There is great blessing in giving and receiving.

POSTSCRIPT

In recent years we've heard much discussion about the different personality types of human beings. One popular notion claims that there are Type A people and Type B people. Type A people are competitive, and Type B people are more reserved. A Type A person will stand in the express lane at the supermarket, the lane where the sign says "Ten Items or Less," and proceed to count the number of items in each person's basket—just dying to confront the person in front of them with eleven items by saying, "Mister, can't you read?"

My wife, Carol, is one of these foot-tappers in the grocery line. She doesn't say anything to them, but she sure would like to. I'm not certain that you can make these generalities about people, but I know that I lean toward Type B while Carol is leaning hard toward Type A.

This difference in us was never more apparent than on a canoe trip down the Hillsborough River just outside Tampa, Florida, a few years ago. We were on a church outing and had nine canoes filled with people. Carol was in the front of our canoe, Lincoln was in the middle, and I was in the back. We shoved off as the ninth and final canoe. Now, my idea of a great canoe trip is to lounge in the back and enjoy the trip. This, however, was not Carol's preference. She saw this as a competition—a race. She was thinking, *We can't be last!* I was thinking,

It would be cool to be last. She was thinking, *We have to get to the end!* I was thinking, *Let's see what we can see out here. Let's take our time and get our money's worth.* She began to instruct us. "Paddle, Bob! Watch out for that limb, Bob!"

Lincoln has some of his mother in him. This presented a serious problem. We now had a mother-and-son Type A team in the front of a canoe. This can be a dangerous thing. They were now glaring at one another, trying to give each other instructions about how to speed the canoe up. But they were trying not to raise their voices too much because there were church folks around. We wouldn't want them to think that the parsonage family was normal, you know. Linc and Carol each had ideas about how this trip should be made, and they were not shy about telling the other. It's funny to sit in the back of a canoe and watch two Type A personalities fight in the front.

Well, I must be honest with you. I didn't enjoy the trip that much. There was quite a bit of fuming and bickering and a lot of raised eyebrows, mostly pointed in my direction for not paddling fast enough. Carol was happy to say, though, that we went from last to finish fourth. I guess the trip was all right, but I was so busy paddling that I'm sure I missed seeing some intricate spider web patterns and a ten-foot alligator lurking just beyond our canoe, and some gnarly cypress formations. Oh, well. We were fourth.

Now this is the part of the trip that amazed me. We got back in the car to go home, and immediately Carol and Lincoln looked at each other and almost in unison said, "Now that was fun!" I couldn't believe it—they had actually enjoyed it! And they had been arguing the whole time. It's hard to figure out a Type A. I'll tell you this, though: I believe they ought to have two kinds of canoes—*competitive* canoes and *contemplative* canoes. I know which one I want to be in.

And I was thinking about you. Sunday after Sunday, month after month, and year after year, you faithfully sit in your place in your canoe—excuse me, *church.* You've been there, no matter your personality, fulfilling your responsibilities as best you can. Sometimes there have been some disagreements. Sometimes there have been some spats and harsh words—but you've been big enough to make it right and keep paddling. You've known instinctively that we need everyone in the family to stick together and keep pulling together.

I thank God for you today. I believe that you're a wonderful layperson. I also believe that God has even greater plans for you. As you live a prayerful, humble, Spirit-filled, positive, generous, faithful life of integrity in your church, God will continue to grow you into the effective layperson He has dreamed you to be. There may be some difficulties along the way, but if you can just keep your eyes on Jesus, you'll enjoy the trip. And in the end, you will have lived a rich, rewarding life.

During World War II one of the most dangerous assignments was to fly aboard B-24 bombers. These noisy, uncomfortable planes had to fly over enemy territory routinely. Many of them didn't return. In his book *The Wild Blue* Stephen E. Ambrose explained that once the soldier had flown thirty-five missions, he had completed his duty and could come home. It was the custom to write home and keep loved ones apprised of the number of missions he had flown.

At the end of the letter, as the soldier signed his name, he would include the number of missions he had completed. He would write something like "Your loving husband, John—16". You can imagine that when a letter came, that wife, with trembling hands, would rip it open, and you know the first thing she would look at. That's right. Her eyes would go to the end of the letter to check out the number. She couldn't wait to read, "Your loving husband, John—35. I'm coming home!"

I've had the privilege of knowing many wonderful laypeople. They're not counting the number of missions in their lives, longing for that magical number when they can cease their labors for God. Rather, everything in their lives, their whole reason for being, is to fulfill the one mission that God has asked them to do. Since Jesus poured out His life for them, they have determined to pour out their lives for Him.

I pray that this is your heartbeat also. I believe it is. Keep paddling—but keep your head up so you can enjoy the trip!

You spend countless hours inside and outside the classroom guiding and mentoring others through life's journey. *Every Paul Needs a Timothy* offers you encouragement as you **spend a few minutes reflecting on your commitment and service to God and the Church.**

Every Paul Needs a Timothy
Blessings for Teachers and Small-Group Leaders
ISBN 978-0-8341-2476-9

www.ingramcontent.com/pod-product-compliance
Lightning Source LLC
LaVergne TN
LVHW010625100826
845148LV00014B/3108

* 9 7 8 0 8 3 4 1 2 5 5 1 3 *